G000049360

RHWNG TEIFI, DYFI A'R DON

GOL. IDRIS REYNOLDS
LLUNIAU IESTYN HUGHES

Argraffiad cyntaf: 2021

ISBN: 9781911584353

Gyda diolch i'r beirdd a pherchnogion hawlfreintiau'r cerddi ynghyd â'u cyhoeddwyr am eu caniatâd i'w cyhoeddi yn y gyfrol hon.

Cyhoeddwyd gan Gyhoeddiadau Barddas
www.barddas.cymru

Mae'r cyhoeddwr yn cydnabod
cefnogaeth ariannol Cyngor Llyfrau Cymru.

Argraffwyd gan Wasg Gomer, Llandysul.

Llun y clawr: Iestyn Hughes.
Dyluniwyd gan Dylunio GraffEG.

Diolchiadau

Carwn ddiolch i:
Gyhoeddiadau Barddas am gomisiwn a oedd wrth fodd fy nghalon;
Iestyn Hughes am ei luniau trawiadol sy'n rhoi dimensiwn ychwanegol i'r gyfrol;
Dylunio GraffEG am greu dyluniad hardd;
Huw Meirion Edwards o'r Cyngor Llyfrau am ei drylwyredd wrth ddarllen y proflenni;
Alaw Mai Edwards am ei gofal a'i hynawsedd wrth lywio'r gyfrol drwy'r wasg,

CYNNWYS

Rhagair

Clywais ddywedyd mai Duw ar y trydydd dydd a greodd y dirwedd ond fod ôl llaw dyn ar y tirlun. Yn y gyfrol hon cawn gipluniau personol o dir a daear Ceredigion, boed dirwedd neu dirlun, trwy lygaid ei beirdd. Mae'r cynfas yn eang a'r ymateb yn amrywio o'r personol i'r gwleidyddol ac o'r hiraethus i'r gobeithiol. Yn wir, nid yw pob un o'r cyfranwyr yn Gardis o ran gwaed, ond gellid dweud mai darn o Geredigion a fu man cychwyn y gerdd a ddewiswyd ar gyfer y gyfrol hon.

Bu Ceredigion erioed yn gyfoethog ei barddoniaeth ac ymdreiddiodd cerddi fel 'Rhos Helyg' gan B. T. Hopkins, 'Ystrad Fflur' gan T. Gwynn Jones a 'Tre-saith' gan Cynan i'n hisymwybod i'r fath raddau nes dod yn rhan o'r olygfa. Cafwyd blodeugerddi ardderchog yn portreadu'r sir trwy lygaid ei beirdd cyn hyn, megis casgliad T. Llew Jones *Awen Aberteifi* yn 1961 a *Cerddi Ceredigion* yn 2003 o dan olygyddiaeth Lyn Ebenezer.

Rhag dyblygu yn ormodol penderfynwyd hepgor caneuon a gynhwyswyd yn y cyfrolau hynny. I chwilio ymhellach am gyfoesedd cyfyngwyd y dewis i feirdd a oedd yn dal yn fyw ar droad y ganrif. Mae'r tirlun diwylliannol a chymdeithasol yn newid yn gyson, a manteisiwyd felly ar y cyfle i gyflwyno gweithiau rhai o'r beirdd newydd sydd wedi camu i'r llwyfan yn ddiweddar gyda'u gweledigaeth ifanc a gwahanol.

Fe ŵyr y twrist diwylliedig fod golygfeydd yn fwy na gwledd i'r llygaid yn unig; maent yn gyforiog o hanes ac o ystyron i'w synhwyro a'u blasu'n hamddenol ar hyd y daith. Nid yw'r golud i gyd yn y golwg. Gobeithio felly y bydd y gyfrol fach hon yn gymorth i chwi werthfawrogi ein sir fwyfwy wrth grwydro rhwng Teifi, Dyfi a'r don.

Idris Reynolds

Cywydd Croeso, Eisteddfod Ceredigion

Su o du'r gors ydyw'r gân
ac ias unig ei swnian
undon yn fferru'r gweundir
a'i hochain hallt a'i chŵyn hir
yn oedi. Hen gân ydyw
drwy'r goedwig, anniddig yw.

Oriog yw ein galaru,
rhy rwydd ein dihidrwydd hy.
Daw ugain ugain yn nes,
ugain ugain a'i neges.
Fesul un, ar ein hunion,
troi sy' raid at wae'r sir hon.

Ym mro'r ŵyl ymwrolwn
hyd y sir, rhaid cadw sŵn
a throi'r rhod; fe ddaeth awr hon –
awr deg i Geredigion,
a daw o'r gors nodau'r gân
i'n gafael drwy'r sir gyfan.

Os ugain ugain yw'n her,
wynebwn bob un aber
o raid, ym mhob stryd a bro
awn ati, hawliwn eto'n
tir yn ôl; rhaid troi ein ha'n
un i'w gofio ... rhag ofan.

... ...

Heddiw, di-liw ydyw'r lôn,
ac aros mae Tregaron,
ond er yr her, gwn daw'r ŵyl
i'w hafan; fe ddaw prifwyl.
Daw'r haf eilwaith drwy'r felan
a su'r gors i g'nesu'r gân.

Gwn daw'r lôn i'n huno ni –
rhoi'r haf 'nôl i'n pentrefi,
yn brawf fod inni barhad,
yn dynnach ein haduniad.
Rhaid i ni ail-lenwi'r lôn
a'n dwg i Geredigion.

Anwen Pierce

Llif Coch Awst

Pan ddeuai llif coch Awst o'r bryniau hyn,
roedd nentydd dirifedi'n bywiocáu
a'r fro yn dal ei hanadl yn dynn.

Pan oedd y caeau gwair yn wag o wyn,
ag ambell wylan unig yn glanhau
y deuai llif coch Awst o'r bryniau hyn.

Roedd cyfnod newydd, gwell, ar ael y bryn,
rhai pethau'n dod i ben, a rhai'n parhau,
a'r fro yn dal ei hanadl yn dynn

fel pe bai dawns ym mrigau'r cyll a'r ynn
o'r cwmwl trymaidd eto'n ymryddhau
pan ddeuai llif coch Awst o'r bryniau hyn.

Disgwyliwn, fel yr hen felinwyr syn
mewn haf breuddwydiol o obeithion brau
y fro sy'n dal ei hanadl yn dynn,

am sŵn y daran gyntaf uwch Moel Llyn,
am gyffro'r rhyddid sydd yn agosáu,
a llif coch Awst yn dod o'r bryniau hyn
i fro sy'n dal ei hanadl yn dynn.

Hywel Griffiths

Llanfihangel dan Eira

(Chwefror 2004)

Drwy'r cwm rhwng y bedw a'r cyll, – ym mhob hafn,
Yn ysgafn, ysgafn, fel curiad esgyll,
Bu'r gwagle'n taenu'i fentyll – yn llen gêl
Ar hyd Llanfihangel dawel, dywyll.

I'n gwlâu oer yng ngenau'r glyn, – yn ei thro
Daeth awr y deffro hyd eitha'r dyffryn:
Mis Bach amhosib o wyn – fel manna,
A gŵyl o eira'n ein gwadd yn glaerwyn.

Haen feddal dangnefeddus – dros fyd dof,
Heb ddim ond brithgof drwy'r plu atgofus
Am bitran patran petrus – y düwch,
Un trwch o dawelwch gwyn hudolus.

Ni allem ond bod allan – drwy'r dydd hael,
Ei gael i'n gafael a'i gael yn gyfan,
Y wlad dan awyr lydan – loyw las,
A'r heli eirias yn orwel arian.

Heddiw roedd ffurf dragwyddol – Eryri,
Fel Llŷn ac Enlli, yn rhithfyd hudol,
A ninnau'n blant ynghanol – ein man gwyn,
Heb un yfory na sôn am feiriol.

Y rhiw a'r llan dan yr un – gyfaredd
A'r cerrig bedd yn wên gam, ddanheddwyn,
Yw cedyrn yn cyrcydu'n – y pant draw,
Hithau'r goedwig ddistaw gerllaw fel llun.

Uwch y coed cylchai cudyll – ei dir gwyn,
Gan ddisgyn ac esgyn fry a'i esgyll
Ar annel tawel, tywyll, – a'i hen brae
O hyd dan warchae ei danio erchyll.

Huw Meirion Edwards

Ar Weun Blaenddôl

(ar achlysur 65 mlwyddiant D-Day)

Gwelais, flynyddoedd maith yn ôl,
Ryw filwr tal ar Weun Blaenddôl,
Ac yn ei law fe ddaliai lun
O fachgen bach fel fi fy hun.
Roedd llygaid gwag y dyn yn goch,
A llifai dagrau lawr ei foch.
Ceisiodd fy nenu ato i'w gôl,
Y milwr tal ar Weun Blaenddôl.

Roedd milwyr eraill llawn cybôl
Yn fawr eu trwst ar Weun Blaenddôl,
Ond sefyll yno wrtho'i hun
Wnâi'r milwr tal a ddaliai'r llun.
Cynigiodd imi degan pren
A losin cnoi a ffownten pen,
Er hynny awn i ddim i gôl
Y milwr tal ar Weun Blaenddôl.

Diflannu wnaeth ar antur ffôl
Un dydd gan adael Weun Blaenddôl,
Efe a'r lleill ar ddydd o ha'
I draeth a enwyd Omaha,
Eu gwaedd ddiflannodd yn y gwynt
Fel gwaedd rhai aeth i Gatraeth gynt.
Ni ddaeth yr un fyth eto'n ôl
O'r milwyr tal i Weun Blaenddôl.

Mae'n dawel nawr ar Weun Blaenddôl,
Ond daw hen atgof di-droi'n-ôl
Weithiau; ar chwyslyd nos ddi-hun,
Gwelaf y plentyn yn y llun,
Hwnnw â'r wên a'r cyrliog wallt,
Yn awr yn wylo dagrau hallt
Wrth ofer ddisgwyl cysur côl
Ei dad, fu gynt ar Weun Blaenddôl.

Lyn Ebenezer

'You're not from these parts?'

Na, dydw i ddim, dwi'n dod o dalaith
ymhell i'r gogledd, a fu'n deyrnas unwaith,
dwi'm yn medru'r acen na'r dafodiaith,
ond pan ddo' i'n ôl i'r fro 'ma eilwaith
yn deithiwr diarth, yn dderyn drycin
a sgubwyd gan y storm, neu fel pererin
yn dilyn y llwybrau o Bonterwyd i Bontrhydfendigaid
fe gerddaf yn hyderus, a golwg hynafiaid
yn cyfeirio fy nhaith, yn llewyrch i'm llygaid;
achos mae pob taith eilwaith yn gwlwm
â'r ddoe sy'n ddechreuad, â fory ers talwm,
ac yn y distawrwydd rhwng dau hen gymeriad
ar gornel y bar, mae 'na filoedd yn siarad
am ffeiriau a chyrddau a chweryl a chariad,
am fyd fel yr oedd hi, am y gweddill sy'n dŵad:
na, dydw i ddim o'r ardal, ond fe fedra' i glywed
clec sodlau y beirdd wrth iddyn nhw gerdded
o noddwr i noddwr, o gwmwd i gantref
cyn dianc rhag Eiddig ar hyd ffordd arall adref:
bûm foda, bûm farcud, yn brin ond yn beryg,
bûm dlws, bûm Daliesin, bûm yn crwydro Rhos Helyg,
bûm garw, bûm gorrach, bûm yma yn niwyg
pregethwr, tafarnwr, breuddwydiwr a bardd,
na, dydw i ddim yn lleol, ond yn y dyfodol a dardd
yn ddwfn yn hen ddaear Pumlumon, ac wrth fynd,
meddai'r henwr o'r gornel, 'Siwrne dda i ti, ffrind'.

Iwan Llwyd

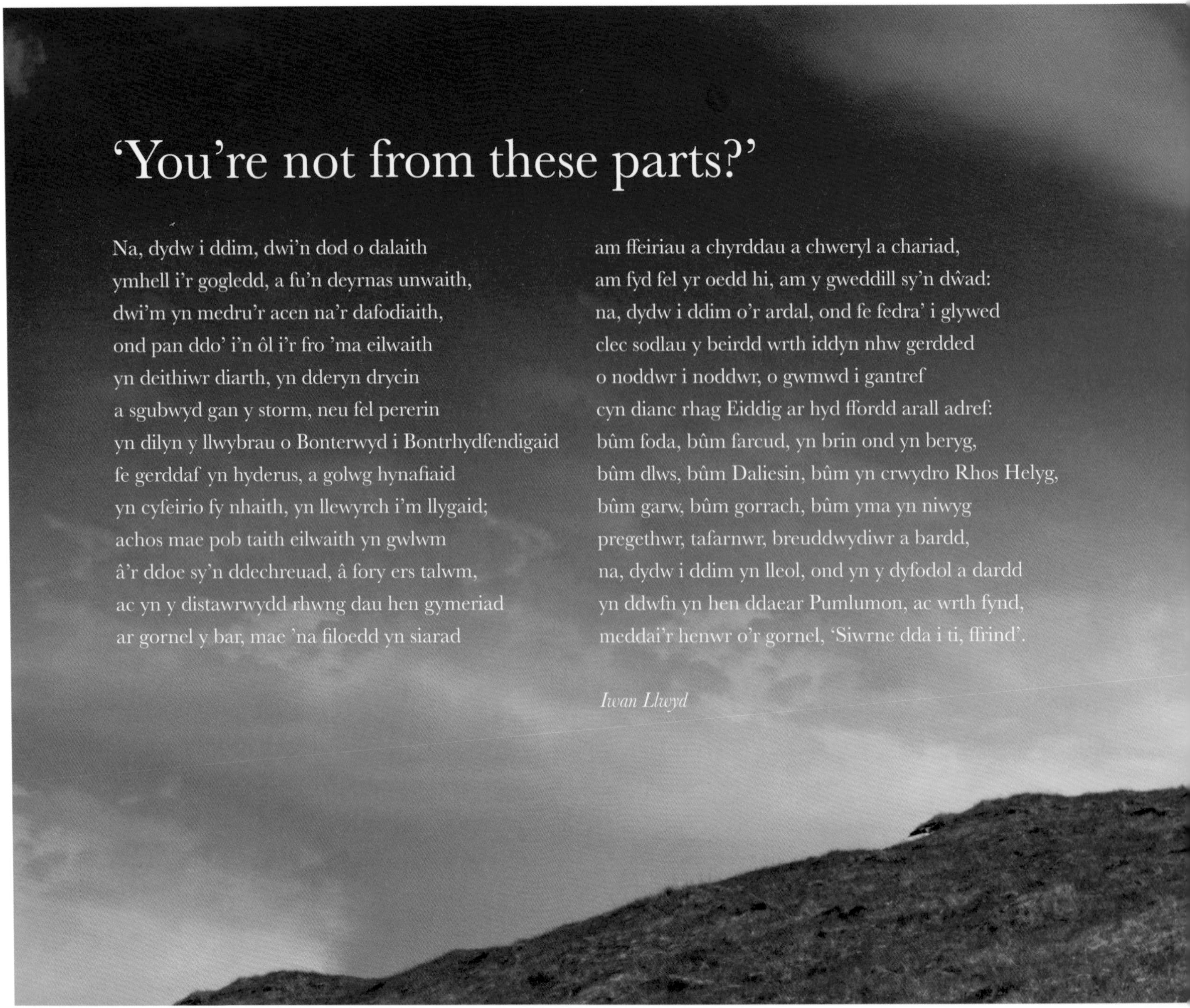

Tyddyn

Mae pobol wrth fy nrws yn curo beunydd
Yn cynnig crocbris am ryw ddarn o gae
I godi tŷ neu 'mofyn hawl drwy'r gweunydd
I gladdu y garthffosiaeth, fel petae.
Mae yma gartws, beudy ac ystabal
Ac ugain cyfer rhwng y ffordd a'r nant
Nad ŷnt fywoliaeth er eu trin yn abal,
Mwynderau mwy na heb i blesio'r plant.
Ond cyndyn wyf i ollwng un cornelyn
O'r etifeddiaeth hon o gyrraedd llaw
Rhag crwydro fel telynor gyda'i delyn
A thant ar goll, yn chwilio am y traw.
Amddifad fyddwn rhwng anhedd-dai'r fro
Heb annibendod buarth, buwch a llo.

Vernon Jones

Cyn y Don Nesaf

(*dolffin ym Mae Ceredigion*)

Chwilio'r bae â llygaid blin, a gweld
Ystwyll ar ganol ha' yn Aberystwyth

– Epiffani, noson o roddion rhyfeddol
a'r pnawn yn pefrio fel papur anrheg plentyn –

Dylan Eildon, baban yr haul a'r heli
yn chwerthin yn dy grud, dy wely gwyrdd
heb fam i suo'th ddagrau ond y tonnau.

Ninnau, yr annoethion, yn nesáu
i osod ein hanrhegion ger dy fron –

ffydd, gobaith, cariad yn gyfnewid
am ennyd o ddiniweidrwydd cyn y don,

cyn y don nesaf.

Elin ap Hywel

Tribannau'r Deuddeg Mis

Ma'r Calan wedi paso
A'r dydd yn dechre stretsho,
Pan fydd hi'n fain ar Fanc Fron Goch
Bydd cawl cig moch i gino.

Ma' rhew ar bylle'r Cefen
A'r sgwarnog wan yn llefen,
Os ffoi i'r tŷ wna'r ci a'r gath
Ma'n wa'th yn Esger Garthen.

Rwy' ofan yn 'y nghalon
Gweld Mowrth yn byta'r wisgon,
Yn wa'th na dim bydd cyrff yr ŵyn
Ar lwyn fel blode gwynion.

Mor neis yw gweld y Glame
A'r geir yn dod i wye,
Os cewn ni ambell flewyn glas
Bydd Penwen mas y bore.

Mis adar bach yn caru,
Mis troi y da o'r boudy,
Mis hela tac, mis bwbach brein,
Mis towydd ffein heb garthu.

Ma' blode ar y ddeiar,
Fe ddaw y tatws cynnar,
Ac i Ffair-rhos am wâc o'r tra'th
Fe dda'th y bilidowcar.

Ma'r lloi a'r da ar gered
Yn dianc rhag y pryfed,
A Wil yn smoco baco shag
I'w gadw rhag y gwybed.

Cerbyde am y cynta,
Dieithred yn pysgota,
A finne'n mynd i Gilfach Rhew
I hela blew gwair cwta.

Ma' min ar fla'n yr awel
A'r glaw yn dal i ddiwel,
Ond os mai Shôn yw bòs pen seld,
Cewn weld Ha' Bach Mihangel.

Ma'r fuwch bron bwrw'i chyde
Am fynd i bori'r adle,
Ni cheiff glofersen o'r Ca' Draw
Nes daw hi'n ddiwedd Hydre'.

Ma'r defed lawr o'r Crynga'
A'r menyn yn y twba,
Ma' llond y pwrs o bishys tair –
Mi af i ffair Clangaea'.

Mor llwm yw Cefen Brosog
A'r gwynt dros Fanc Ca' Madog,
Bydd caib a rhaw y ceib'wr tal
Rhwng peder wal y 'Nachlog.

W. J. Gruffydd

Iet y Plas

At yr iet daw eto'r un – i aros
yn chwarae haf plentyn,
â'i Awst drwy'r bwlch yn estyn.

Rhywle rhwng un lle a'r llall – mae rhaniad
mor anodd ei ddeall,
a dôr at ryw fyd arall.

Er y mur, er yr ymyrraeth, – a'i glawdd,
mae'r glwyd yn gynhaliaeth
a'i chadwyn yn warchodaeth.

Byw gwledig, bod â digon, – byd elw,
a bodolaeth estron
yw pob darn o'r harn yn hon.

Er y drain a chwa'r dwyreinwynt – weithiau
ddaw i wthio drwyddynt,
barrau du o barhad ŷnt.

Trwy'r allt daeth crwt yn alltud – o'r tu fas
i'r iet fawr am ennyd,
at haf cyfalaf o fyd.

Yn y cloeon mae e'n clywed – hoelion
ei dylwyth yn cerdded,
galw mae Ffosrhydgaled.

Yna trwy'r adwy wedyn – hwn a wêl
yn heulwen y llecyn,
hen arfer ydyw terfyn.

Geraint Roberts

Arfordir

Ei chlywed wnes, o bell
yn chwerthin gyda'i chriw,
ei llais yn gyllell
trwy wynt y môr.

Safwn innau yno
yn gwrthod symud,
yn gwrthod coelio
bod hon a'i North Face drud
yn gwarafun bro fy mebyd.

Syllais arni,
pwyso'n nes at destun ei sbri:
TRAETH WALLOG 1/4 MILLTIR

'What does that even mean?'
Jyngl o lythrennau,
cawdel ar bostyn pren.

Dau lwybr oedd,
dau ddewis yn oes oesoedd.

I lawr i'r traeth yn dawel,
yn ddall, yn ddiddeall,
ymddiheuro mwy neu lai
am drybini dybryd ein bod
cyn oedi, ar y tir draw
i glicio, tapio,
postio'r profiad ar byrth y we.

Dyma'r stwff sy'n tanio'r dydd.

Llwybr serthach oedd y llall
yn nadreddu'n droellog
tua'r clogwyn
lle byddai'n rhaid dringo,
chwysu, cydio yn y cerrig llac
i ddangos i hon a'i chriw
bod y tonnau'n dal i dorri
ar draeth ein hiaith
islaw.

Dal ati wedyn
dros y twyni, heibio'r dibyn
a theimlo'r hesg yn gwau'n hanesion
yn rhaffau praff am ein coesau,
lle daw hithau trwy'r heli
i holi
pwy'n union oedd y Brenin,
a Seithenyn, a'i strach?

Oddi yno, eu tywys
gan bwyll bach,
yn griwied bodlon, parod
hyd y lôn i lawr i'r Sarn
lle daw hithau yn ei *selfie*
i ryfeddu
at ruddin dwfn
y boncyffion brau.

Dau lwybr oedd,
dau ddewis yn oes oesoedd.

Oedais, cyn mentro ati,
roedd hon yn haeddu gwybod
nad yno i ddangos y ffordd
y mae'r arwyddion

ond dangos hefyd ein llwybrau,
ein hanes, a'n holion.

Megan Elenid Lewis

Y Ffenest at y Fynwent

(detholiad)

Mae 'na lot o sôn am Aberystwyth –
yn enwedig am y babi-newydd, druan bach, sy'n 'druan bach'
am fod arno angen help i'w fwydo a'i fatho, i fynd ag e am dro
mewn pram mawr du ar hyd y prom, a chanu 'Si-hei-lwli-'mabi'
iddo fe bob nos. Gan nad oes sôn am 'helpu newid cewyn' –
y busnes diflas hwnnw sy'n rhan o fod yn fami, ond nid o fod
yn gnither fowr, gobeithio – mae hi'n gwirfoddoli'n llawen,
a'i dwy chwaer, hefyd, wedi styried tipyn.

Rhaid pacio'r cyffro yn y cesys:
pajamas a sandalau, siorts a dillad nofio, hetiau haul ac eli –
holl anghenion gwyliau haf.
Drannoeth – y bregeth fer arferol:
'Joiwch. A bihafiwch.
A halwch garden bert.'

A'r codi llaw o'r ffenest yn pellhau nes bod yn sbecyn
ar ffenest gefn eu tacsi dierth, cyn diflannu'n llwyr.

... ...

Rhyfeddodau'r haf:
y prom prysur, y pwll padlo, y golff gwallgo,
parc chwarae'r castell, trên Constitution Hill,
cornets pinc y Pengwin, traethau Ynys Las
a'r Borth – popeth braf dan haul Awst,
yng nghwmni'r 'laughing policeman' ar y pier:
'Ha-ha-ha-ha-ho-ho! Oh! I'll laugh until I die!'

Derfyn haf yn 'Aeron'
roedd y gwely mawr yn wag.

Dyna'r drefen, a rhaid ei derbyn.

Manon Rhys

Môr a Mynydd

Mae Llŷn mor agos heno, ac mae'r byd
yn crwydro hyd y Prom; cariadon chwil
yn sibrwd fel yr haul, a chaeau ŷd
yw'r tonnau'n siffrwd yn y Bae, a mil
a mwy o straeon a hanesion sydd
i'w hadrodd a'u hailadrodd ddechrau ha',
a phawb yn chwilio'n astud am ryw ffydd
o hyd, fel plant â'u gwenau hufen iâ.
Mae Llŷn mor agos heno, ond yr un
yw'r pellter heddiw ac yfory; does
ond symud disymud y dŵr, a'r llun
fan hyn yn newid dim o oes i oes.
Mae'r tonnau'n llepian y copaon pell
a phobol hyd y Prom yn cyfarch gwell.

Dafydd John Pritchard

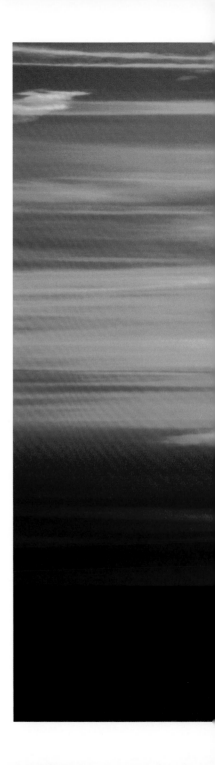

ACHUB
PANTYCELYN
Prifysgol
Celwydd Cymru
Save
Pantycelyn
Prifysgol
Celwydd Cymru
Prifysgol
Celwydd Cymru
Prifysgol
Celwydd Cymru
Save
Pantycelyn
ACHUB
PANTYCELYN
Save
Pantycelyn
ACHUB
PANTYCELYN

Neuadd Pantycelyn

(yn ddeg ar hugain oed yn 2004)

Yn dri deg mae'r anrhegion
Yn o sad, yn ôl y sôn.
'Travel clocks' a socs o'r sêl,
Stwff glanhau a dau dywel,
Mỳg lle bu jỳg, a 'jogging
Shoes' a 'blues' lle bu 'bling-bling'.

Yn adeg y dyledion
Heneiddiodd hi'r neuadd hon.
Yn oedran codi gwydrau
I diwn nad yw'n mynd yn iau,
A yw'n amser i gerrynt
Iach y sîn barchuso'i hynt?

Ydio ddiawl! Nid rhyw gawlio
Mae Panty na cholli'i cho',
Nid yw Nawr yn mynd yn hen,
Ni ddaw neuadd ein hawen
I'w hoed-'i byth tra ceidw'r
Presennol llethol ei llw.

Oni chlywch o wal uchel
Y Ffynnon ni'r dynion del
Yn canu'n llac yn ein llys?
Canu am fory'n farus
A chanu coch yn y Cwm
Fu'r llys Dilys ers talwm.

Ni all rheol ffôl na ffi
Na'r un pwyllgor cynghori
Noddi neuadd ddiniwed
I'r rhain ar lawr neu ar led.
Adeilad i wehilion,
Noddi hwyl mae'r neuadd hon.

Cwyd, pan ddaw Derec wedyn,
Cwyd yn blaen o'i flaen fel hyn –
Cwyd fys o boced y Fall,
Cwyd fys hir, cwyd fys arall,
A chwyd y ddau uwch dy ddwrn
Ac ysgwyd croen ac asgwrn!

Ond efe ni wêl dy fys
Oni weiddi'n gyhoeddus
Blydi hel! o'th blaid dy hun
Ac o blaid y cwbl wedyn.
Os cwd, cwd ifanc ydwyf,
Cyfiawnhau y cyfan wyf.

Yn Sycharth, os yw achos
Owain yn oer, os yw'r nos
Yn Aberffraw yn dawel –
Mae llu ym Mhanty'n ymhél!
Beth yw tranc? Ifanc yw'r co'
Presennol parhaus yno.

Neuadd gre', ddigri yw hon,
Neuadd, ogof o ddigon,
Neu fil o glyd ogofâu
Yn ei labrinth o lwybrau,
A thyrau braf ei hafiaith
Yw tyrau aur geto'r iaith.

Ond nawdd od y neuadd hon,
Neuadd lwyd o ddyledion,
Yw bod ei holl aelodau
Â dim i'w wneud ond mwynhau.
Nid tŷ nad un heb ei do,
Nid byd, byd heb *libido*!

Yn nydd rhifo'r neuaddau
A rhoi rhif ar werth parhau,
Yn nydd dy enwi o hyd
Yn ifanc eto hefyd,
Os dydd dy barchuso di,
Deg ar hugain dy grogi.

Eurig Salisbury

Cyrraedd Aber

a pharcio'r car.
llafnau gwydr ar y gwynt

yr un yw'r plant ar risiau'r
capel, yr un yw'r sgyrsiau
wrth y drws; yr un
yw'r môr a'r adar mân

yr un yw'r dyn, a'i gân
yn siffrwd tywod hyd y pafin

yr un yw'r gwely oer
a'r gegin, a'r daith o un
i'r llall, a'r disgwyl.

Gadael Aber

... ac wedi dweud popeth sy'n weddill i'w ddweud
mi awn ni i bacio, am na allwn ni wneud

yr un dim am yr amser sy'n dŵad o hyd
i ddanfon yr adar ar ffo dros y byd.

Iestyn Tyne

Cofiwch Dryweryn

Daw'r gwanwyn awr yn fwynach
i wawrio byd adar bach,
hwy'n prysur dwtio muriau
o frwynen i frwynen frau,
wrth igian hen gân i'r gwynt –
un haid yn dweud pwy ydynt.

Eu cân sydd yn eu cynnal
er i rai falurio'r wal,
dod fin nos a difa nyth
ac aelwyd eu gwehelyth,
yn troi hwn yn fur ein tranc,
... ond dyfal yw'r to ifanc.

Aled Evans

COFIWCH
DRYWERYN

Pontydd

(*detholiad*)

Ryw eiliad cyn i'r heulwen
glwydo heno'n wylan wen,
o'r dref oer fe grwydraf i
ymylon afon Teifi.
Ac o'r bont lle llusga'r byd
daw'r haf gyda'r dŵr hefyd.
Mehefin o sewin sydd
yn llenwi'r pyllau llonydd.
Islaw rhwng llus o liwiau,
i bwll hir yn ymbellhau
yn y gwyll, pluen o gwch
yn hwylio ar dawelwch.
A gerllaw mae gŵr a llanc
yn eu hafon yn ifanc
yn dala dwy wialen
a blaen hir y bluen wen,
gan enweirio'r gân araf
yn yr hwyr dan awyr haf.

Dwy wialen yn pendilio'n araf
dros y dŵr digyffro.
Diferion mân sy'n glanio'n
ddafnau cwyr ym mhyllau'r co'.

Tad a mab, hawdd adnabod – o wyneb,
ôl y genyn hynod.
A natur yn annatod
yw llinyn bywyn eu bod.

Eu llinach ydyw'r llinyn; – hen edau
cyndeidiau yn estyn
o enynnau y ddau ddyn,
edau eiddil rhwng deuddyn.

Eto, wrth nesáu atynt,
dau lais sydd mor dawel ŷnt;
dau yn swil gyda'i gilydd
a dau ŷnt fel nos a dydd,
ar ddwy geulan wahanol
a dŵr ddoe yn hollti'r ddôl.

A heno, dan Bont Einion – y dŵr llyfn
y daw'r llif atgofion,
yn y gwyll fel brithyll bron
yn nofio yn yr afon.

Gwenallt Llwyd Ifan

YR HEN BONT 1805 THE OLD BRIDGE
Y BONT NEWYDD 1972 THE NEW BRIDGE

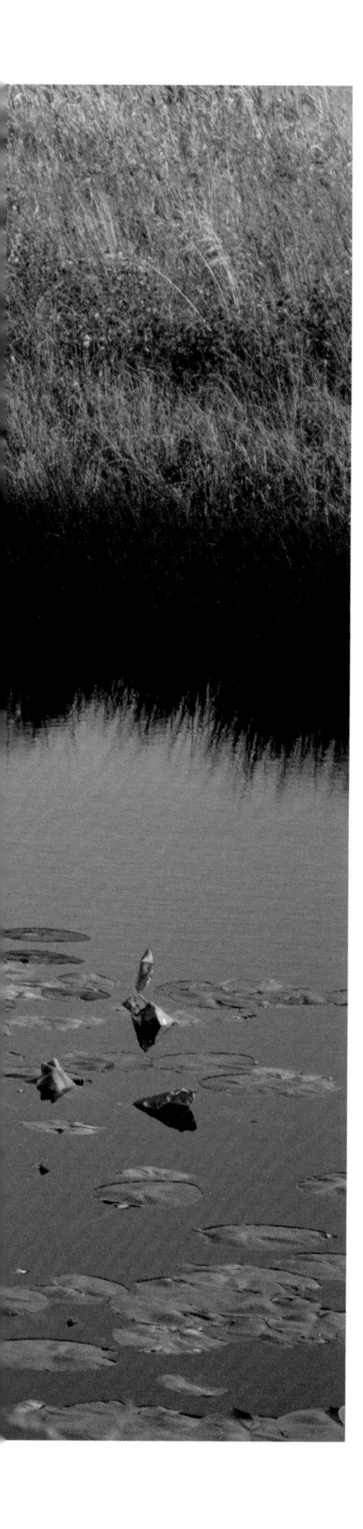

Y Gors

O ddirgelwch
  y gors wrth lannau Teifi
cyn hollti'r frwynen,
  bu'r brain yn dilygadu'r ddafad
yn ffos ei hangau gwlanog,
  a'r broga'n drachtio'r merddwr
wrth dwmpathau'r brwyn.

Yn nyfnder iraidd y gors
  storiwyd drwy'r canrifoedd greiriau'r oesau:
celanedd cof,
hynafiaethau hil,
yn haenau ar haenau archaeolegol
  yn amgueddfa'r ddaear.

Er cyn cof,
  onid gwallgof y gors?
A llarpiwyd yn llysnafeddog
weddillion coed a briwydd y cynfyd;
  yn y migwyn gwelais y llygod
yn llygadrythu
i lygaid newynog eu tranc,
ac ymysgaroedd y lysard
  ar chwâl fel tegan yfflon wrth geulan y rhyd,
a'i gwaed fel crawel y gelynnen
uwchlaw'r dŵr.

Pair cof ydyw'r gors,
  crochan y dadeni oesol
sy'n ffrwtian chwedlau
  ein maboed,
    ein cynddaredd
      a'n greddfau gwyllt,
cyn i'r edling
  dreisio'r wyryf synhwyrus,
ryw nos
        yng ngenau'r ogof.

Islwyn Edwards

Banc Rhydeinion

Ar frig y rhos arhosant,
Ar wyneb bryn y parhânt
Tan y diwedd, y gweddill
Yn byw o'u swcr a phob sill
O'r heniaith sy'n gwrteithio
Daear cae a dyfnder co'.

Olion gwrol hen geyrydd
Uwch y sarn o'u hamgylch sydd;
Rhyw gladdau mawr, gwelydd maith
Ddoe hanes fu'n nawdd unwaith:
'Does neb wrth Lawen heno
Yn nwfr rhyd er mwyn y fro.

Yno y maent yn ymhél
Â bywyd drwy bob awel;
Yno ymysg 'sgyrion main
Tyddynnod dydd eu hunain,
A'r estron o Saeson sy'
Ar eu hannel yn prynu
Yr hen dai di-raen, diwerth
A'r ffermydd rhydd sy' ar werth.

Duw a roes fywyd i'r rhain
Yma'n eu nythfa noethfain
I'w rhuddin i ymwreiddio
Yn wybr wydn a phridd eu bro
Nes bo'u cof yn troi'n brofiad,
A braint eu dyfalbarhad
Yn ddawn yng nghraidd eu henaid
Drwy'r gwynt ar eu hynt o raid.

Nid hen ddynion mohonynt
Hwy oll ar derfyn eu hynt,
Y mae 'na barau ieuanc
Yn byw er Byw ar y Banc.

Donald Evans

Breuddwyd

Â'i lygaid-cyfri-praidd yn tremio draw
fe saif ar glos ei deidiau'n dal ei dir
â Ffan a Moss o'i ddeutu'n llyfu llaw.

Ei gap sgi-wiff yn herio, haul neu law,
wrth iddo fân frasgamu 'nghamre'r gwŷr
â'i lygaid-cyfri-praidd yn tremio draw.

Cans gŵyr heb orfod ateb unrhyw braw'
fod cwlwm dyn a daear yno'n bur
â Ffan a Moss o'i ddeutu'n llyfu llaw.

Y borfa'n llonni i gennad cog, a'i thraw
yn rhithiol ddenu aer yr erwau ir
â'i lygaid-cyfri-praidd yn tremio draw.

Gorwelion ei wanwynau'n ddi-ben-draw
wrth greu ei rwn ei hun ar wndwn hir
â Ffan a Moss o'i ddeutu'n llyfu llaw.

Holl ddoeau ei hil yn swyn y fory a ddaw,
yn seithmlwydd o hynafgwr gwêl yn glir
â'i lygaid-cyfri-praidd yn tremio draw
â Ffan a Moss o'i ddeutu'n llyfu llaw.

Huw Evans

Cynefin

Dyma'r lle
y taenwyd llieiniau
yng Nghae Llain
ar hyd cloddiau;
yng Nghae Pistyll
dan y dderwen
dringo yno
ar bob cangen.
Porfa'r gwanwyn
gwair a llafur,
yno gweled
gwyrthiau natur.
Dyma'r byd
i ailddarganfod
pelydrau'r haul
ar dir Cymreictod.

Golau sydd
yn deffro'r lliwiau,
llunio'r paent
mewn llu gweadau.
Lliwiau llachar
byd plentyndod
yn atgofion
yr anwybod,
a chydio'n llaw
y lluniau yno,
sydd yn bell
yng nghell fy nghofio.

Aerwen Griffiths

Soar-y-mynydd

Tra ffald yn gartre i ffydd, un neu ddau
ddaw o hyd yn ufudd
yma i hel yr awel rydd
a'r emynau o'r mynydd.

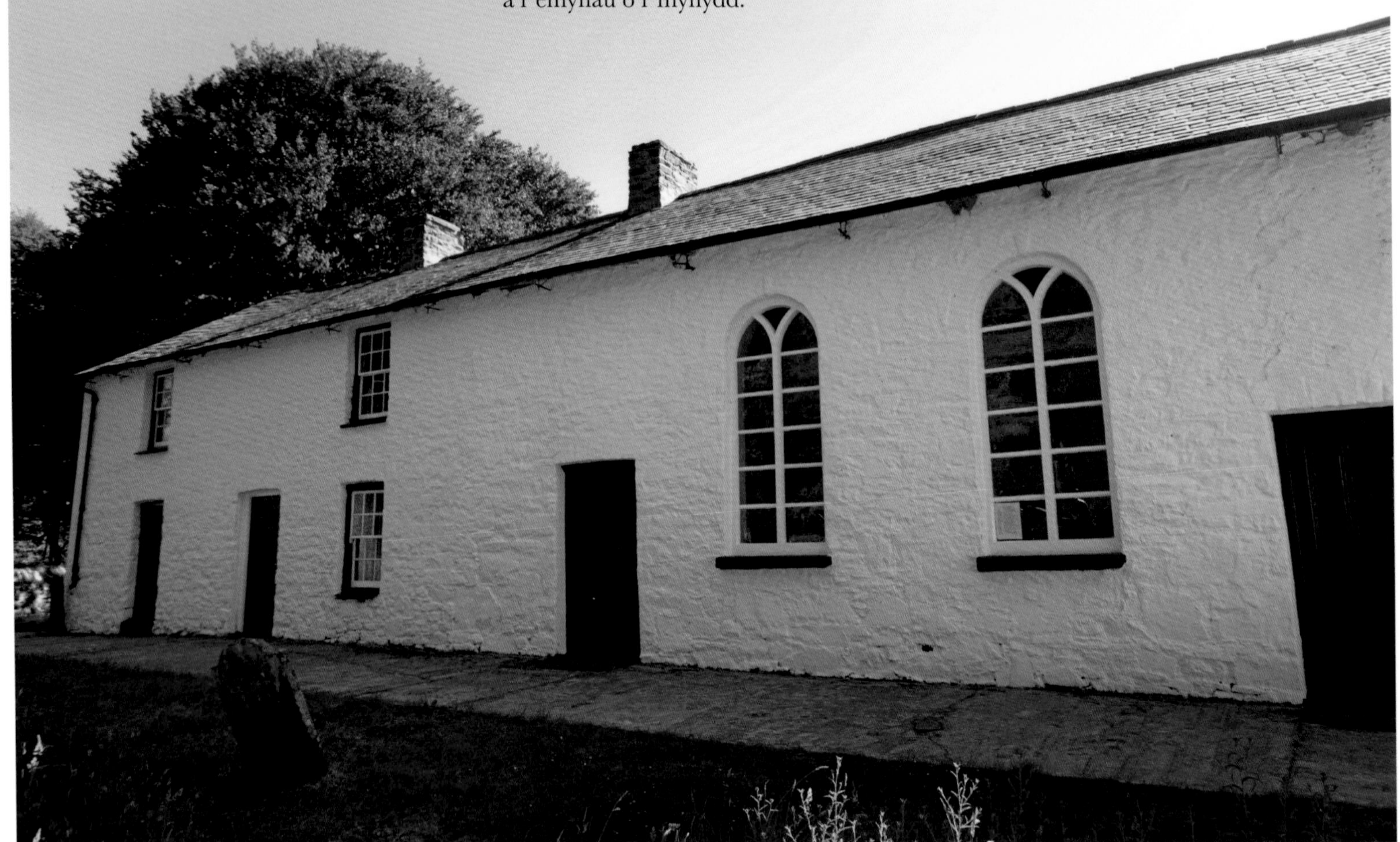

Trên

(y llinell rhwng Aberystwyth a Chaerfyrddin)

Yn y stesion hon, er blino aros
    ers yn hir amdano,
  ar y trac, tu hwnt i'r tro,
  ei hwtian glywaf eto.

Yr Hen Ffatri Wlân

Caled fu gweled cilio yn y cwm,
a gweld cau'r holl gyffro,
ac mae'r garthen sydd heno
drosof i yn cosi'r co'.

Endaf Griffiths

Ennill Tir

(detholiad o'r gerdd er cof am yr Athro Hywel Teifi Edwards, Aber-arth)

'Ddaw 'na neb? 'Fyn 'na neb nawr
galennig ddygwyl Ionawr?

Twt! 'Does na chrwt na chroten
â sill pennill yn eu pen.
Neb â'i fryd ar hybu'i fro.
Neb â iaith i obeithio.
Ni ddaw'n rhwydd inni'r flwyddyn.
Ni fyn neb ddod i fan hyn.

'S neb 'lan? 'Oes 'na neb 'leni?
'Fyn 'na neb ofyn i ni
euro'i law ar ŵyl a oedd
ddoe'n bennill, heddiw'n bunnoedd?
'Ddaw 'na neb. 'Fyn 'na neb nawr
galennig o law Ionawr.

Ai heb wyneb yw Ianws?
Onid yw'r wawr wrth y drws?
Ac eira fel y garreg
onid yw dwy fil a deg
yn gri ac ynddi hen goel
am fargen lem ofergoel?

Yn Aber-arth, do, bu 'rio'd
galennig, fel gwylanod:
drwy'r plwyf fe raeadrai'r plant
yn firi o lifeiriant,
a'u chwerthin yn golchi'n gân
ddyddiau celyd, ddydd Calan.

Dylifent, drwy'r tai, nentydd
o fawl i'r fordaith a fydd,
a rhoi ym min pentre'r môr
foregan dros fyw ragor.
(Os hŷn na gras ein hen gri,
hŷn ein goddef na'n gweddi.)

Y cyntaf draw i'n cyntedd
yn glyd ei glod a gâi wledd.
A châi côr neu denor da
droi atom i ladrata!
Ond pob dyn, pob un a'i bill
a gâi geiniog, ac ennill.

Rhyfedd o fyd! Hyd yn hyn
fe lwyddwyd bob un flwyddyn.
Llanc y llynedd – lle heddiw?
Lle egni'i droed? Lle'i gân driw?
'Fyn na neb ofyn i ni?
Bwceidiem ei bocedi!

Tudur Hallam

i
CEREDIGION

Ffermwyr Ifainc Ceredigion

Nhw yw'r hwyl mewn gŵyl a gwaith, – nhw yw'r côr
Sy'n rhoi cân ein gobaith,
Acen ifanc ein hafiaith
Yn rhannu hoen â'r hen iaith.

Nhw a'u dawn sy'n dihuno – y ddaear
A'i haddewid eto;
Nhw'r ynni brwd drwy ein bro,
Nhw'r gwanwyn ar egino.

Dylan Iorwerth

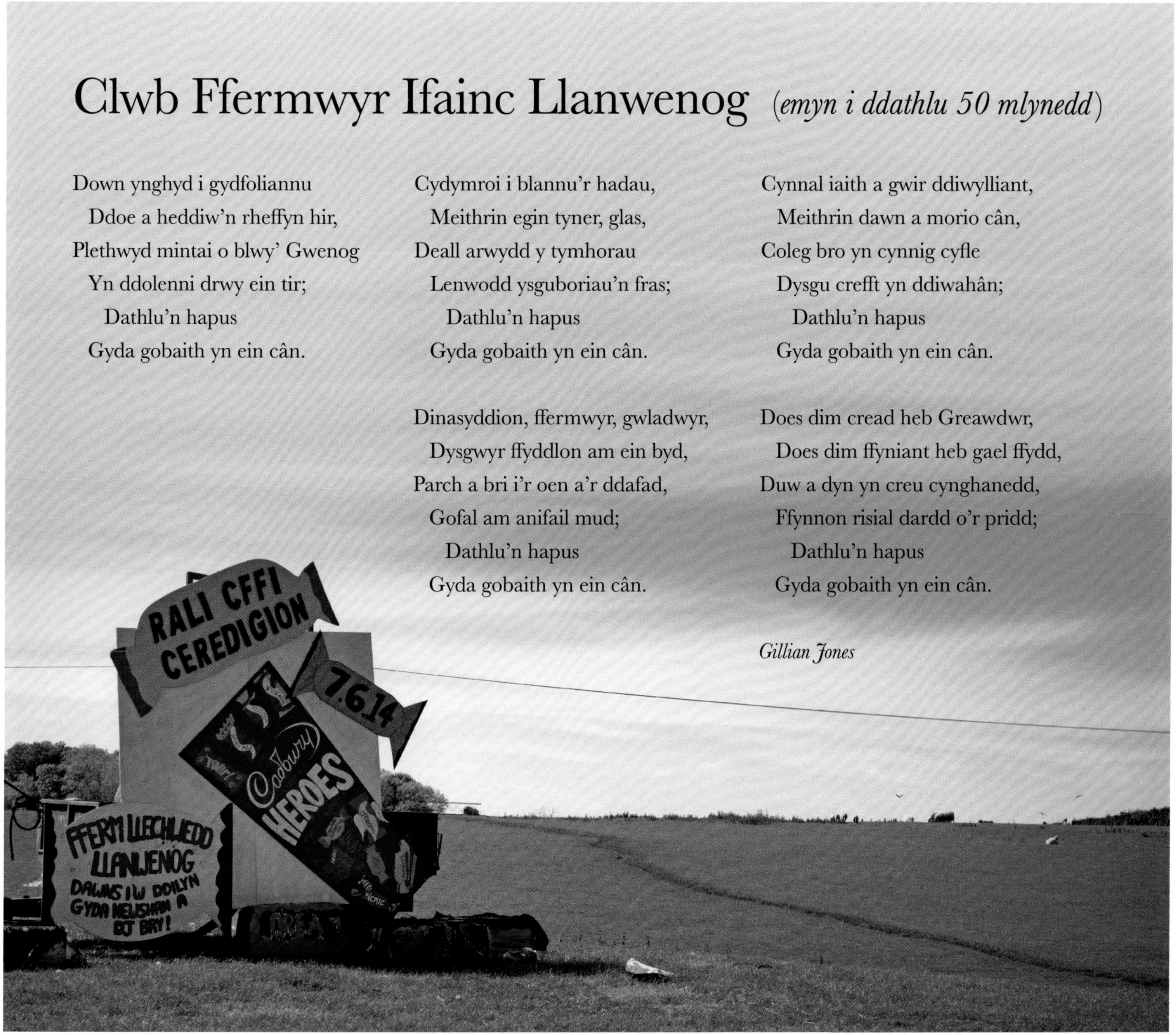

Clwb Ffermwyr Ifainc Llanwenog *(emyn i ddathlu 50 mlynedd)*

Down ynghyd i gydfoliannu
  Ddoe a heddiw'n rheffyn hir,
Plethwyd mintai o blwy' Gwenog
  Yn ddolenni drwy ein tir;
    Dathlu'n hapus
  Gyda gobaith yn ein cân.

Cydymroi i blannu'r hadau,
  Meithrin egin tyner, glas,
Deall arwydd y tymhorau
  Lenwodd ysguboriau'n fras;
    Dathlu'n hapus
  Gyda gobaith yn ein cân.

Cynnal iaith a gwir ddiwylliant,
  Meithrin dawn a morio cân,
Coleg bro yn cynnig cyfle
  Dysgu crefft yn ddiwahân;
    Dathlu'n hapus
  Gyda gobaith yn ein cân.

Dinasyddion, ffermwyr, gwladwyr,
  Dysgwyr ffyddlon am ein byd,
Parch a bri i'r oen a'r ddafad,
  Gofal am anifail mud;
    Dathlu'n hapus
  Gyda gobaith yn ein cân.

Does dim cread heb Greawdwr,
  Does dim ffyniant heb gael ffydd,
Duw a dyn yn creu cynghanedd,
  Ffynnon risial dardd o'r pridd;
    Dathlu'n hapus
  Gyda gobaith yn ein cân.

Gillian Jones

CO-OPERATIVE STORES
PENUWCH

Ymweliad

(ymweliad â Bear's Hill, Penuwch, Mai 2009; er cof am y Prifardd John Roderick Rees)

Er bod y dodrefn yn yr un drefn
a'r llyfrau'n yr un lle
â deugain mlynedd ynghynt,

roedd y lle tân newydd mor ddierth
a di-dân â'i drem.

Dechrau procio lludw'r cof
a'i atgoffa
o'r crwt a ddeuai
â'i gerddi eisteddfodol, sâl ar nos Suliau;

o'i dad yn ailgered mewn geiriau
ei farch cyn belled â Brecon;
a Jane, yn porthi o gwmpas ei phethe

ac o sŵn y Brenin, y cobyn, yn ceibo
yr ochor arall i'r wal.

'Mae dy lyged di'n sbarclo nawr, Jack,'
meddai'r ofalwraig ffeind wrth y ford,
ac yntau nawr fel Jane ei gerdd gynt
'yn braidd-gyffwrdd â glan'.

Ac er i'r golau ddiffodd yn llwyr
ar aelwyd 'yr ynys ddiddan',
dim ond i chi agor clawr y gorwel
fe ddeil y geiriau i fflachio,
i gipoleuo hen fyw gwledig, i guro'n galon ystyfnig,
i'n hatgoffa – a'n rhybuddio
oddi ar Enlli
ei gerddi e.

Cyril Jones

Angladdau Llambed

'Yn y dyfroedd mawr a'r tonne'
ddaeth ar donfedd rhyw ben bore,

minnau'n swrth rhwng cwsg ac effro,
a waeth na dim, ar hanner siafio.

Yna mi glywais dyner lais
y gweddus, barchus Cerdin Price

yn sôn yn ddwys am gyfrifoldeb
wrth drefnu'r daith i dragwyddoldeb.

Does dim byd mwy fel y buodd e
a'r trefniant yn newid o le i le,

cewch gatalog i wneud eich dewis
o Gary Glitter i Ann Griffiths,

wrth dalu 'mlaen cewch 'special rates'
o ddrws y ffrynt i'r 'Pearly Gates',

gall Mair y Forwyn a Chalfaria
rannu'r llwyfan 'da Madonna,

Bassey, Lulu, Elvis, Elfed
a Phantycelyn ar y pamffled.

Nid Calon Lân i galon drom
ond hwyl Deleila gyda Tom.

Mae Craig yr Oesoedd dan fy nhraed
a 'Rock and Roll' yn poethi'r gwaed.

Caf felodïau Pantyfedwen
mewn 'Green, green grass' o dan yr ywen,

ac O! mor bêr ar ddydd y glanio
fydd craclan miwsig wedi'i ganio.

Dafydd Lloyd Jones

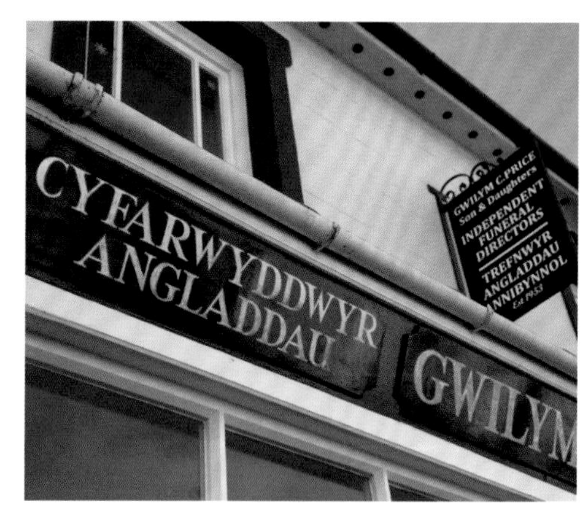
CYFARWYDDWYR
ANGLADDAU
GWILYM
GWILYM C.PRICE
Son & Daughters
INDEPENDENT
FUNERAL
DIRECTORS
TREFNWYR
ANGLADDAU
ANNIBYNNOL

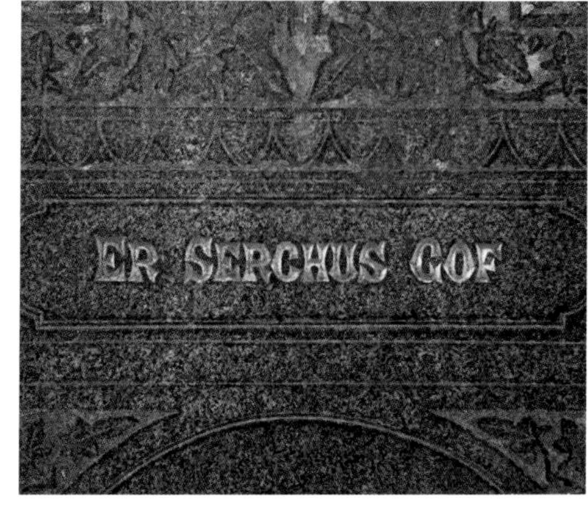
ER SERCHUS GOF

Cymydog

Lan ar yr hafod, yn edrych i lawr
ar y machlud a'r pentre. Mae cysgod ysgall
wedi ymestyn hyd hanner cae.

Sŵn chwiban a defaid fel afon wen
yn rhaeadru drwy'r gatiau, yn ddyfroedd byw.
Beth yw perthyn ond perthi sydd yn cau

dieithriaid allan? Mae'r dof yn werthfawr.
Stoc y tu mewn, a'r diwerth gwyllt
mas ar y gweunydd. Dyw cymuned glòs

ddim yn cynnwys pob enaid. 'Gwyliwch chi,'
meddai'r ffarmwr wrth gau'r glwyd yn glep,
'mae'n beryg bywyd ar eich pen eich hun

ar y mynydd. Mae'r bwystfil ...' Ar ba ochr o'r clawdd
y mae ef? Osgo cyfarwydd. Mae'n galw ar ei gi
a rhegi. Ar ba ochr o'r gwrych rydw i?

Gwyneth Lewis

Llygaid

(detholiad)

Ysgol fach ar ben y rhiw,
Goroesodd y chwalwynt.
Bonnie, merch a fwriodd y diwreiddiedig wynt
I'r hafan hon,
I'r stafell Gymraeg ac O.M.
Yn dal i deyrnasu ar y mur.
Dieithrwch y Geltiaith yn tyfu'n gynefin
Ar wefusau cymysgiaith.
Plant nad yw Offa'n eu geiriadur
Yn cymuno a chyd-fyw
Drwy Esperanto'r ysbryd.

Lucy fach â'r cyfenw estron
Yn 'Dysgu Tedi'
Ar lwyfan cyngerdd
A gofyn 'Pwy sy'n dod dan bont y glaw?'
Ar iard yr ysgol.
Areithio'n dwt yn y Cwrdd Tri Misol.
Hwn yw'r testament newydd yn ein gwaed.

Hebddynt ni byddai yma
Ond tomen sgrap hen deuluoedd,
Magwyrydd yn frech
Ar gnawd y gweunydd;
Adfeilion wedi'r malu.
Menter parau ifainc yn cyweirio cyfannedd,
Adnewyddu hen dai,
Aileni hen grefftau.
Dwylo estron yn trin gwlân a lledr,
Crasu bara, gwadnu a chlocsio:
Ymrithio eilwaith o'r hetwyr a'r gwydrwyr gynt,
Cynheiliaid y ddoe a ddarfu.

John Roderick Rees

I Euros Lewis

(i'w gyfarch ar ei ymddeoliad o Theatr Felin-fach)

Codaist dy deml Roegaidd
yn y Dyffryn, a'i hurddas
ar dafod leferydd Cymru gyfan.

Creaist ddelweddau'r duwiau
gan eu dwyn yn fyw ar lwyfannau'r fro.

Rhyddheaist y ddawn wâr gan sicrhau
cadarnle i ddychymyg lifo
o adain i adain hyd y llen olaf.

Buost lusern, a'r *deus ex machina*
yn gelfydd yn dy stori.

Buost yn llamhidydd yr arena,
a'th weledigaeth yn atseinio
drwy'r cynteddau at dy ddilynwyr triw.
Buost ddawn ddigri, ddifrifol
gan ddatgelu'r cyfrinachau o gainc i gainc.

Agoraist y llen ar gymeriad o fro,
ei goslef tu draw i ddrama unnos,
a'r Dyffryn yn llafarganu yn un corws.

Cerddaist hyd lwyfannau'r creu
a thywys Aeron fel llawforwyn
i ddenu'r llawryfon.

Buost yn glust i wrando
ar lef ddistaw fain dy famiaith
gan ei thywys yn ôl i'r canol llonydd.

Boed i'th ddawn eto ddisgleirio
a'th grefft gryfhau, er mwyn
gwarchod y deml yn y Dyffryn
a adeiladwyd gennyt
mor gelfydd, mor gyndyn.

Ann Rhys Davies

Cobiau Sadwrn Barlys

(sioe geffylau ar strydoedd Aberteifi yn niwedd Ebrill yn dwyn lluniau'r arlunydd Aneurin Jones i gof)

Heddiw, mae'r wlad a'i hadar
yma'n segura'n y sgwâr:
hwn-a'r-llall yn llenwi'r llan
yn lleuadau cefn llydan,
yn cellwair â'u ffyn collen
a'u capiau, fel hwythau'n hen;
yn poeri'r ateb parod
sy'n sbort yn eu sgwrs, nes bod
y dre'n wlith o straeon lu,
yn hewl fawr o lefaru.
Wynebau dŵr a sebon
a'r hen wlanen biau'r lôn.

Er bod meirch ifanc, ceirchiog
ar hyd y stryd fel stŵr og,
er bod gambo'n gwisgo'i gêr
a chel mewn bràs a choler
a'i rawn a'i fwng yn crynu,
nid â dawns ei flewyn du
â'm hanadl ond am ennyd
a'r palmantau'n gobiau i gyd.

Myrddin ap Dafydd

Terfysg

(*detholiad*)

Map (Arolwg Ordnans Rhif 198)

Uwch cilgant deudraeth
taenaf fap uwchben y môr

a gosod pedair carreg ar ei gyrion
rhag y gwynt.

Mae map yn blingo gwlad
hyd esgyrn ei chlogwyni,
hyd rydweli ffordd,
gwythïen meidr.

Dyma lawfeddygaeth tir,
trem farwol o'r entrychion;
fertigo.

Ar y tipyn papur hwn
mae cyfrinachau:

i'r gorllewin, tu hwnt i'm gorwel,
yr orynys
sydd mor gudd â Gwales;

ac o Graig Filain fwyn hyd Bencribach –
i fyny ar ororau'r map –
rhes o byramidiau coch
yn parthu'r bae'n
faes perygl,

lle'r arferai'r *Pheasant*
a'r *Eliza Jane*
dorri cwys â'u cargo calch,

llwyth cwlwm eu carennydd,

... ...

Glasach ei glas

Bob haf,
dilynem hynt yr afon Saith
o'i mabinogi yn y ffos o byllau brag
ym Mlaensaith Fawr

i'w phrifiant yng nghysgodion Dyffryn Saith

hyd foment fawr ei hymwacáu
yn bistyll ger y traeth –
dŵr
yn torri'n darth
ar ddŵr,

naid afon
'nôl i goflaid môr.

Trwy gryndod golau Awst
galwaf ar y plant, a chodi llaw;

tynnu'r sbectol haul
i brofi'r syndod,

dyfnder, bendith
awyr wag.

Damian Walford Davies

Dau Fod Mewn Car

(i Meilyr)

Gwibio heibio Glynarthen
di-liw yn y glaw
a meddwl heb feddwl,
'bues i'n byw fan'na
cyn dy fod di.'

Cododd storm,
'cyn fy mod *i*,' meddit,
ond sut oeddit *ti'n* bod
os nad own *i*;
a ble own i ta beth?'
a dyw geiriau fel cwmwl awydd
ddim yn denu dy ddiogelwch;
na sôn am hadyn heb ddod i groth
fel taflu brigyn i afon
a'r disgwyl troellog at lan môr
yn mennu dim.

Rhewynt rheswm sy'n para.
Meddit eto,
'os nad own i eto'n dy fol
oedd un gyda ti?'

Y bach na ddeall Drefen
mor fawr
(fwy na finnau)
ond yn ailddysgu'r sawl
a 'fu' cyn iddo e 'fod'

mai ei fyw e yw geni'r fam.

Menna Elfyn

Pentref

(*Llangrannog yn y gwanwyn*)

Heddiw
gwelais y gwanwyn
yn daclus
heb bêl yn agos
i sgwaryd clecs y dail.

Cerddais hyd glogwyni
a chlywed cân y gwersyll
yn hofran dros dro
uwch Lochtyn ...

Drws tŷ yn gwichian,
a chwpwl crwm
yn sgwrio'r gaeaf yn hamddenol
oddi ar eu trothwy diarth.

Dof yn ôl,
Dof yn ôl â'm plant
i fyw stori
Cwmtydu,
cwrso geiriau
mewn ogofâu
a'r dyfodol yn draeth.

Heno,
mae fy straeon eithin gwyllt
yn staen ar ffenest.
Rwy'n poeri fy iaith
ddyrys
ar wynebau poléit
fydd yn aros
trwy'r gloch olaf.
Unig wyf
ar stepen oer
yn rhannu ffag gyda'r gwynt,
yn gweiddi geiriau
mewn cragen
am fod y machlud wedi ei brynu
a'r dyfodol yn dywodyn.

Dof yn ôl.
Dof yn ôl
drwy'r broc môr
i fagu, i fyw
efallai ...

Mari George

Gŵyl Nôl a Mla'n, Llangrannog

Un gronyn o Langrannog
a'n try'n ôl i'n Tír na nÓg
a'i ogof o atgofion.
Yr haf a'r Urdd yw'r fro hon
i'n co', lle bu'r tro i'r traeth
yn anadl i'n hunaniaeth –
a Bica'n rhoi ei hanwes
i ni; lle deuem yn nes
trwy fân siarad; bu'n adeg
''da'n gily' mewn tywy' teg'.
Gennym bu grym geiriau rhydd
o gilio at ein gilydd.

A Bica'n dal ein hanes,
nawr yr Ŵyl sy'n rhoi in wres
cwmnïaeth, ar draeth a dry
yn wlad drwy adeiladu
llwyfan iaith – a llifwn 'n ôl
i'r gad, o wlad lai hudol.

Fe fyn ein torf angorfa'n
y fan hallt, a'i hufen iâ'n
felys, gan droi'n hynys ni'n
uniaith, am unwaith, inni.
Heddiw, mae'n plant ar 'sgwyddau,
a'n cân sy'n eu bywiocáu
mewn bro sy'n ceincio encil
â phob cytgan a chân chwil.

Ym Mae'r eigion mor agos,
daliwn dir yn hir, hyd nos
a dan nesáu, cadwn sŵn
yma, heno, lle mynnwn
oedi'r haul, rywfaint, dros dro
a chael hud y machludo.

Philippa Gibson

CARLING

PENTRE
ARMS

TAFARN-Y-LLONG
THE SHIP INN

Drych

Heno, yng Nghenarth,
Yn y dŵr oer gwelais drem
O fy wyneb fy hunan.

Ond yn y dŵr
Nid llun yn unig
A nofiai ar afon Teifi
Mewn rhyw bwll sydd islaw meini'r bont,
Waeth tu ôl i'r llyfnder yn y dyfnder du
Gwelais o fin y geulan
Fy mywyd i gyd, a gweld
Y miloedd o gymylau
Ar war y nos yn crynhoi.

Yn y dŵr yr oedd stori,
Yn y dŵr – fy mywyd i
A welais am eiliad.

Yn Nheifi roedd yr hyn a anghofiais
Yma yn fy ymyl.
Ond pwy yn y cyfnod pell
A wnaeth ddweud wrth ddŵr
Afon Teifi
Am aeaf a haf fy oes?

Aeth rhyw wefr ddieithr iawn
Yn iasau drosof.
Yna'n sionc brasgamais i
O ymylon yr afon ryfedd
A'i drych a godai ryw ofn
Heno yng Nghenarth.

Dai Rees Davies

Tre-saith

Darfu yr Awstiau hirfaith
ar y swnd ym mae Tre-saith
lle bûm ger y pyllau bas,
neu'n erlid tonnau irlas.
Roedd llethr uwch dadwrdd y lli
a dyrnaid o dai arni
a'u hoedl oedd fel cragen dlos,
cragen ymhlith caregos.
Ond y trysor a dorrwyd
gan ferw y llanw llwyd;
gwnaed cofeb o bentre bach,
o gymuned, gwymonach.

Emyr Davies

caffi a siop fforest
fforest store & cafe

Dim ond Cymrâg Aberteifi sy 'da fi

'Dyw Nghymrâg i'n ddim i'w bragian (yn nhre'r
Arglwydd Rhys o bobman)
wa'th hi yw'r iaith ar wahân
yn ei *ghetto*'n bigitian.

Mae o'i chof, mae'n ei hofon am aros
rhwng y môr a'r afon;
iaith hen granc yw ei thiwn gron,
iaith anghŵl, iaith angylion.

Hi yw'r iaith ym Mron-y-dre; iaith yr Hope,
iaith Rhiw Ropeyard hithe;
iaith y capel ar sbele;
iaith â'r jiawl – ac iaith Ridgeway.

Iaith brics coch, iaith bracso cân; iaith y Red,
iaith y rhwydi'n gwegian;
iaith ôs a wês, iaith y Sân;
iaith y pitsio, iaith potsian.

Iaith boi'r hewl, iaith y browlan; iaith seiens,
iaith sewin mewn ffrimpan;
iaith codi hwyl, iaith gwylan,
iaith dŵr Mwnt, iaith adar mân.

Iaith p'nawn gwlyb, iaith pannu gwlân; iaith y tir,
iaith teras yn cloncan;
iaith rhaffu, iaith yr effian,
iaith ofyrôls, iaith y frân.

Iaith cowbois ac iaith cobie a bwrlwm
Sadwrn Barlys ynte;
iaith iobs drwg, iaith bois y dre;
iaith y Gotrel, iaith gytre.

Iaith Fflach ac iaith heb swache; iaith Llandoch
(ac iaith Llunden weithie);
iaith wag i rai – ond iaith gre',
yr iaith i'r dysgwyr hwythe.

Iaith y bobol, iaith baban; iaith gobaith
o'r Gwbert i'r Mwldan;
iaith agor iet, iaith â gra'n,
iaith hen win, iaith 'n hunan.

Ceri Wyn Jones

Lleisiau

(detholiad o 'Porth yr Aber')

Y mae hollt yng nghraig y môr
A rhwyg, fel porth ar agor,
Yng ngodre bae fy mebyd,
Ac aber ers bore'r byd,
A mainc lle trochionodd môr
Yr oesau'n deidiau didor
O gylch trwyn, a golchi traeth,
Drwy'i ddiwydrwydd, yn ddeudraeth.

Dygai swnd ei gysondeb
I loywi ael carreg wleb –
Rhygnu'r cregyn o'r creigiau
Ac i fewn i'r ogofâu,
A llyfnhau â llif ei nerth
Genfaint y creigiau anferth,
Nes naddu'n gyson iddynt
Fan i gwch o fin y gwynt.

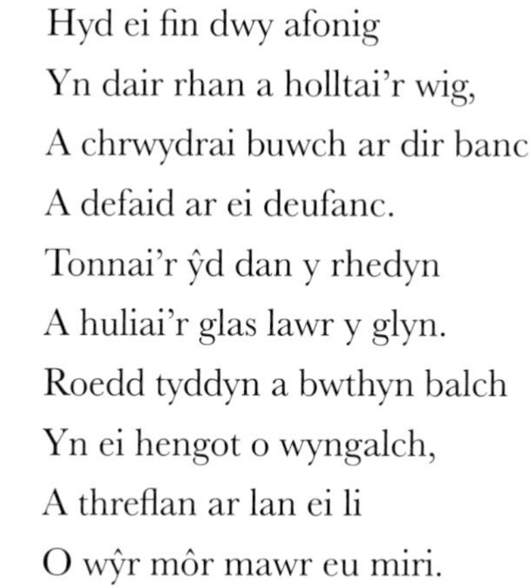

Hyd ei fin dwy afonig
Yn dair rhan a holltai'r wig,
A chrwydrai buwch ar dir banc
A defaid ar ei deufanc.
Tonnai'r ŷd dan y rhedyn
A huliai'r glas lawr y glyn.
Roedd tyddyn a bwthyn balch
Yn ei hengot o wyngalch,
A threflan ar lan ei li
O wŷr môr mawr eu miri.

Dic Jones

Ceredigion Môr a Thir

Gwlad Ceredig a'r meysydd glas,
Llwybrau tawel a'r afonydd braf,
Mae'n galw ni heddi fel yr oes o'r blaen, yr oes o'r blaen;
O Soar y Mynydd i Ystrad Fflur,
Llefydd o addysg a myfyrdod pur,
Rhai o hyd yn pregethu'r Gwir, pregethu'r Gwir ...

Cytgan
Ceredigion môr a thir:
Mae'n annwyl iawn i ni,
Dewch yma cyn bo hir.
(*ailadrodd y cytgan*)

1176 daeth Arglwydd Rhys
Â'r Steddfod gyntaf i'r dre ar y ffin,
Yn Aber mae 'na drysorau di-ri, trysorau di-ri;
Ger Cors Caron mae'r Barcud Coch
A natur yn serennu'n y fro,
Mynyddoedd Cambria mewn urddas a hedd, urddas a hedd ...

Traethau Aber-porth a Thre-saith
A dolffiniaid yn y bae,
Ac Eglwys Mwnt dyw hi byth ar gau, byth ar gau.
Cranogwen oedd arwres ei dydd
Ar y llongau yn teimlo'n rhydd,
Y Frythones oedd ei llwyfan hi, ei llwyfan hi ...

Cytgan

Richard Jones

Caffi'r Emlyn, Tan-y-groes

Gwesty John yw'r lle bonedd:
Arlwy o hyd ydyw'r wledd
Ar y bwrdd, a gwelir beirdd
Yn yfed ymysg prifeirdd.
Wisgi neu gwrw casgen
O'r lle hwn sydd yn creu llên.

Mae hwyl mewn gwinoedd melys
I'r llesg o seleri'r llys,
A'r medd yn curo moddion –
Da yw joch o westy John.
Yn Nhan-y-groes mae croeso,
Tyr y rhew i'r swil bob tro.

Buan y gwan fydd yn gwau,
Fel y gwâr, ei fil geiriau.
John, i ni, ti yw y tad
A ni'n deulu d'adeilad.

Emyr 'Oernant' Jones

CAFFI EMLYN
TANYGROES
SHED HEAD
San Miguel
SOMERSBY
ORIGINAL

Eglwys y Mwnt, Ebrill 1940

Lle chwery'r don ar draethau aur,
Lle clywir trwst y gwynt,
Aeth plant y glannau ati 'nghyd
I godi eglwys gynt.

Es innau yno un prynhawn,
I'r eglwys ger y môr,
Gan adael holl ofidiau byd
Yn aros wrth y ddôr.

Hen Eglwys Mwnt, os Duw a'i myn,
Dof eto'n ôl i'th fro,
I dreulio awr a phethau'r byd
Yn angof oll am dro.

Eglwys y Mwnt

(ar ymweliad â'r fangre dros hanner can mlynedd yn ddiweddarach)

Yn y Mwnt y mae o hyd – adeilad
  I dawelu'r ysbryd;
 Lle i ddod o boendod byd
 Yn ôl at fy anwylyd.

Addurnwaith celfydd arni – ni welir,
  Nac ôl dwylo'r meistri;
 Dim ond symledd tŷ gweddi
 A harddwch ei heddwch hi.

Diysgog gartref crefydd, – hen le'r mawl
  Uwchlaw'r môr a'i stormydd;
 Sêl y saint i'w seiliau sydd,
 Grym y Gair yw'r magwyrydd.

T. Llew Jones

Dic

Roeddem yno mewn tipi
fel *designer hippies* yn breuddwydio
am berthyn drwy lesmair mwg,
a ninnau ar gaeau'r Hendre
lle mae perthyn i'w arogli ar y gwynt,
rhwng dagrau'r môr a choflaid y tir.

Dest i dendio ar dy lysiau
a'th gynhaeaf olaf wedi bod.
Roedd olion yr aredig ar dy ruddiau
a nerth dy eiriau yn dy ddwylo
wrth i dy gorff gynganeddu ei ffordd
ar draws y buarth.

Fe'th wyliais di'n chwynnu'r pridd
o gylch dy sgewyll, heb adael dim
amherffeithrwydd, fel taset yn gofalu fod
sillaf olaf hir-a-thoddaid yn ei lle.

Ond bellach nid oes englynion
yn tyfu yn y tir,
a'u gwreiddiau'n gadarn
i fwydo'r to nesaf.

Ry'n ni nawr yn cynaeafu'r haul
i fwydo'r ddinas fawr
lle mae *haikus* o dramor i'w cael ar silffoedd
wedi eu lapio'n *airtight* mewn plastig.

Fe welaist hyn yn dod; y gwynt
ei hun yn cael ei ddal gan ddyn,
gweld y budd, a gweld y golled,
gweld y tir yn diflannu o dan ein traed ...

Aneirin Karadog

Traeth Cwmtydu ym Medi

(i Jon Meirion, a aeth â ni yno)

Mae'r traeth yn wag. Tawedog yng Nghwmtydu
mwy yw'r Gymraeg ym murmur trist y trai;
mae'r môr dihidio wedi hen erydu
y graig y torrwyd arni enwau'r rhai

a ddôi fan hyn, cyn i'r beddfeini'u henwi
(hyd nes i'r glaw erydu'r garreg lefn
fel môr ar draeth). Er i'w chwedloniaeth lenwi
daear a chof, ni ddônt yn ôl drachefn.

Yma, ar Ddydd Iau Mawr, o gylch yr Odyn,
a'r môr unieithog yn eu hannog hwy,
y doent o hyd. Ai dim ond un tywodyn
yn hollt rhwyf Tydu yw'n treftadaeth mwy?

Mae'r traeth yn wag, a'r môr, ar ein hanogaeth,
yn bwyta rhagor, rhagor, o'n tiriogaeth.

Alan Llwyd

Dydd Gŵyl y Banc

Bydde'n well 'da fi orwedd dan *German tank*
Na bod yn Nhre-saith ar ddydd Gŵyl y Banc.
Mae'r lle yn llawn Brummies, Geordies a Jacks
A menywod Treforys a'u chwech *lager-packs*.
Maen nhw'n eistedd trwy'r dydd yn siarad â'u cŵn
A'u teganau digidol yn cadw sŵn.
Mae'r pentre fel syrcas yn llawn dop o *freaks*
Gyda'u radios a'u *jetskis* a'u plant yn llawn *cheeks*.
Trôns nofio Britannia a *deckchairs* San Siôr
A chwyno bob munud fod y dŵr yn rhy ôr,
Parcio 'mhob man ar leins melyn dwbwl
A chael tocyn dwyieithog a gwên am eu trwbwl,
Gorlenwi y Ship gyda'u gweiddi a'u stŵr
Ac yfed y dablen sy'n fawr gwell na dŵr,
Talu crocbris am bitsa a tsips wedi rhewi,
Mae'n Dachwedd bron iawn cyn i'n pentre ni dewi.
Wy'n meddwl symud i Brighton Gŵyl y Banc
Gyda bws llond mwncïod o'r sw,
A chael pleser o'r mwya 'da'r Saeson bach neis
Wrth wneud yr un peth iddyn nhw!

Dewi 'Pws' Morris

Bywgraffiadau

Myrddin ap Dafydd
Sylfaenydd a pherchennog Gwasg Carreg Gwalch. Fe'i magwyd yn Llanrwst ac erbyn hyn mae wedi ymgartrefu ym Mhen Llŷn. Enillodd ddwy Gadair genedlaethol ac ef yw Archdderwydd Cymru ar hyn o bryd.

Elin ap Hywel
Bardd a chyfieithydd sydd bellach yn byw yn Llanilar. Fe'i ganwyd ym Mae Colwyn a'i magu yn Llundain a Wrecsam. Bu'n gweithio fel cyfieithydd i'r Amgueddfa Genedlaethol yng Nghaerdydd ac i'r Academi Gymreig.

Ann Rhys Davies
Yn enedigol o sir Gaernarfon, ymsefydlodd yn nyffryn Aeron ers dyddiau coleg. Fel athrawes ac addysgwraig, bu'n amlwg yng ngweithgareddau diwylliannol yr ardal, yn enwedig yn Theatr Felin-fach. Bu farw yn ifanc yn 2014.

Dai Rees Davies
Bardd a arhosodd ymysg ei bobl yn ei filltir sgwâr yn Rhydlewis. Bu'n aelod o dîm Ffostrasol ar raglen *Y Talwrn* bob blwyddyn ers i'r gyfres gychwyn yn 1979. Bu'n enillydd cyson mewn eisteddfodau taleithiol a chenedlaethol. Bu farw yn 2019.

Damian Walford Davies
Fe'i ganwyd yn Aberystwyth ac ar hyn o bryd mae'n Ddirprwy Is-ganghellor Coleg y Celfyddydau, y Dyniaethau a'r Gwyddorau Cymdeithasol ym Mhrifysgol Caerdydd.

Emyr Davies
Yn enedigol o Aber-porth. Bu'n ddarlithydd yng Ngholeg y Drindod, Caerfyrddin, ac erbyn hyn mae'n swyddog arholiadau Cymraeg i oedolion gyda CBAC. Mae'n dalyrnwr ac ymrysonwr adnabyddus.

Lyn Ebenezer
Newyddiadurwr, cyflwynydd teledu a golygydd sydd bellach wedi llywio dros gant o lyfrau drwy'r wasg. Erbyn hyn mae wedi dychwelyd i'w bentref genedigol ym Mhontrhydfendigaid ar ôl treulio blynyddoedd yn byw yn Aberystwyth.

Huw Meirion Edwards
Fe'i magwyd yn Llanfair-pwll ac yng Nghaerdydd ond mae bellach wedi ymsefydlu yn Llandre. Bu'n uwch-ddarlithydd yn Adran Gymraeg Prifysgol Aberystwyth cyn ymuno â'r Cyngor Llyfrau fel Pennaeth yr Adran Olygyddol. Enillodd y Gadair genedlaethol yn 2004.

Islwyn Edwards
Yn enedigol o Ffair-rhos. Cyn ymddeol bu'n diwtor Cymraeg i Oedolion yn y Ganolfan Iaith ym Mhrifysgol Aberystwyth ac mae'n dal i fyw yn yr ardal.

Menna Elfyn
Mae'n un o'n beirdd amlycaf a'i hapêl yn rhyngwladol. Dros y blynyddoedd bu'n cyflwyno ei cherddi mewn gwyliau llenyddol ar draws y byd. Bu'n byw am gyfnodau yng Nglynarthen, Penrhiw-llan a Llandysul cyn symud i Gaerfyrddin.

Aled Evans
Fe'i ganwyd yng Nghydweli. Bu'n athro ysgol yn Llandysul ar ddechrau ei yrfa ac erbyn hyn mae'n Gyfarwyddwr Addysg Bwrdeistref Nedd ac Afan. Mae'n aelod o Ysgol Farddol Caerfyrddin.

Donald Evans
Enillodd y Gadair a'r Goron yn Eisteddfodau Cenedlaethol Wrecsam (1977) a Dyffryn Lliw (1980). Erbyn hyn mae wedi ymddeol o fyd addysg ac yn dal i fyw yn ei ardal enedigol yn Nhalgarreg.

Huw Evans
Bardd a bridiwr defaid o ardal Cwrtnewydd. Mae'n enillydd cyson mewn eisteddfodau taleithiol, yn yr Eisteddfod Genedlaethol ac yn y Sioe Fawr yn Llanelwedd.

Mari George
Fe'i magwyd ym Mhen-y-bont ar Ogwr a deil i fyw yn y cyffiniau. Mae'n olygydd sgriptiau gyda'r BBC, yn gyfieithydd, yn llais ac wyneb cyfarwydd mewn gweithgareddau llenyddol ac yn aelod o dîm Aberhafren ar raglen *Y Talwrn*.

Philippa Gibson
Yn enedigol o Fryste, symudodd i ardal Llangrannog yn 1987. Mae ganddi Ddoethuriaeth mewn Seicoleg ond wedi dysgu Cymraeg daeth yn Diwtor Cymraeg i Oedolion. Dysgodd gynganeddu gan ennill ar yr englyn ddwywaith yn yr Eisteddfod Genedlaethol.

Aerwen Griffiths
Athrawes o ardal Llanfair Clydogau. Treuliodd y rhan fwyaf o'i hoes yng Nghanolbarth Lloegr cyn dychwelyd i'w bro enedigol ar ôl ymddeol, lle mae'n cael cyfle i ddatblygu ei thalent fel arlunydd.

Endaf Griffiths

Bardd ifanc a fagwyd yng ngogledd sir Gaerfyrddin ond sydd bellach yn byw ar fferm ger Cwrtnewydd ac yn gweithio ym myd llyfrau. Mae'n weithgar iawn gyda Mudiad y Ffermwyr Ifainc.

Hywel Griffiths

Brodor o Langynog sydd bellach yn byw yn Llanbadarn Fawr. Mae'n uwch-ddarlithydd yn Adran Ddaearyddiaeth a Gwyddorau Daear Prifysgol Aberystwyth. Enillodd y Goron genedlaethol yn 2008 a'r Gadair yn 2015.

W. J. Gruffydd (Elerydd)

Un o feirdd Ffair-rhos a fu'n weinidog gyda'r Bedyddwyr drwy ei oes. Enillodd y Goron genedlaethol yn 1955 ac yn 1960, ac ef oedd Archdderwydd Cymru rhwng 1984 ac 1987 (ei enw barddol oedd 'Elerydd'). Bu farw yn 2011.

Tudur Hallam

Bardd cadeiriol Eisteddfod Genedlaethol Blaenau Gwent a Blaenau'r Cymoedd yn 2010. Mae'n enedigol o Rydaman ac ar hyn o bryd yn ddarlithydd ac yn Athro yn Academi Hywel Teifi ym Mhrifysgol Abertawe.

Gwenallt Llwyd Ifan

Brodor o Dregaron sydd bellach yn byw yn Nhal-y-bont. Bu'n bennaeth mewn ysgolion yng ngogledd a chanolbarth Cymru ac erbyn hyn mae'n hyfforddi darprar athrawon yn Ysgol Addysg, Prifysgol Aberystwyth. Enillodd y Gadair yn Eisteddfod Genedlaethol Môn yn 1999.

Dylan Iorwerth

Newyddiadurwr, awdur a bardd sydd wedi ymgartrefu yn Alltyblaca yng Ngheredigion ers blynyddoedd lawer, lle bu'n olygydd gyfarwyddwr cwmni *Golwg*. Mae'n un o'r ychydig sydd wedi ennill y Gadair, y Goron a'r Fedal Ryddiaith yn yr Eisteddfod Genedlaethol.

Ceri Wyn Jones

Fe'i ganwyd yn Welwyn Garden City a'i fagu yn ardal Aberteifi, lle mae'n dal i fyw. Ef yw meuryn y rhaglen radio *Y Talwrn* ar BBC Radio Cymru. Mae ganddo ddwy Gadair genedlaethol ac un Goron.

Cyril Jones

Brodor o Bennant sydd bellach yn byw yn ardal Pontypridd. Bu'n gweithio fel tiwtor Cymraeg a darlithydd mewn Ysgrifennu Creadigol ym Mhrifysgol Morgannwg. Enillodd y Goron genedlaethol yn Eisteddfod Ceredigion, Aberystwyth, yn 1992.

Dafydd Lloyd Jones
Fe'i magwyd yn Ffair-rhos ac enillodd ei fywoliaeth fel cyfreithiwr yn Llanbedr Pont Steffan. Bu'n aelod o dîm Llambed ar *Y Talwrn* a daeth yn adnabyddus am ei hiwmor crafog. Bu farw yn 2019.

Dic Jones
Treuliodd ei oes yn ffermio tir y teulu ym Mlaenannerch. Enillodd y Gadair genedlaethol yn 1966 gydag un o'r awdlau gorau erioed, ac yn dilyn hynny daeth yn ffigwr cenedlaethol. Bu farw, yn ystod ei dymor fel Archdderwydd, yn 2009.

Emyr 'Oernant' Jones
Ffermwr a bardd gwlad o ardal Aberteifi. Datblygodd yn ffigwr poblogaidd, ffraeth ei ateb, ar lawr *Y Talwrn* ac ar lwyfan y Babell Lên yn yr Eisteddfod Genedlaethol. Bu farw yn 2018.

Gillian Jones
Mae'n dal i fyw yn ei bro enedigol yn ardal Llanwenog. Treuliodd flynyddoedd fel athrawes Gymraeg yn Ysgol Uwchradd Tregaron ac ar ôl hynny fel ymgynghorydd addysg yng Ngheredigion.

Richard Jones
Cerddor o Aberteifi sy'n dal i fyw yn y dref. Gyda'i frawd Wyn sefydlodd y band Ail Symudiad yn 1978 a chwmni recordiau Fflach yn 1981. Ail Symudiad yw'r grŵp pop cyntaf i berfformio ar y Maen Llog.

T. Llew Jones
Fe'i ganwyd ym Mhentre-cwrt yn sir Gaerfyrddin a threuliodd ei oes fel athro ysgol yng Ngheredigion cyn ymddeol i fyw ym Mhontgarreg. Enillodd y Gadair genedlaethol ddwywaith a daeth i amlygrwydd fel awdur llyfrau plant. Bu farw yn 2009.

Vernon Jones
Fe'i magwyd yn Bow Street ac mae'n dal i fyw yn yr ardal. Bu'n gweithio ar y tir cyn ymuno â staff y *Cambrian News*. Mae'n enillydd cyson mewn eisteddfodau lleol, taleithiol a chenedlaethol.

Aneirin Karadog
Bardd, perfformiwr, cerddor ac ieithydd sydd bellach yn byw ym Mhontyberem ond sydd hefyd wedi byw yn Llydaw. Fe'i magwyd yng nghymoedd y De ac enillodd y Gadair yn Eisteddfod Genedlaethol Sir Fynwy yn 2016. Bu hefyd yn Fardd Plant Cymru.

Gwyneth Lewis
Fe'i magwyd yng Nghaerdydd ond mae ganddi gysylltiadau agos gyda Llanddewibrefi. Mae'n barddoni yn Gymraeg a Saesneg a hi oedd Bardd Cenedlaethol cyntaf Cymru. Enillodd Goron yr Eisteddfod Genedlaethol yn 2012.

Megan Elenid Lewis
Merch fferm o Lanfihangel-y-Creuddyn sydd yn newyddiadurwraig a chyfieithydd. Enillodd y dwbl, sef Cadair a Choron Eisteddfod Clybiau Ffermwyr Ifainc Cymru, yn 2018.

Alan Llwyd
Bardd, ysgolhaig a beirniad llenyddol sy'n hanu o Ben Llŷn yn wreiddiol. Ers blynyddoedd bellach mae wedi ymgartrefu yn ardal Abertawe ac ar hyn o bryd mae'n Athro yn Academi Hywel Teifi ym Mhrifysgol Abertawe.

Iwan Llwyd
Bardd a cherddor a fagwyd yng Ngharno, Dyffryn Conwy a Bangor. Yr oedd ganddo hefyd gysylltiadau teuluol ar ochr ei fam gydag ardal Brongest yng Ngheredigion. Ef oedd enillydd y Goron genedlaethol yn 1990. Bu farw yn 2010 yn 52 oed.

Dewi 'Pws' Morris
Canwr, cerddor, digrifwr ac actor sy'n llais ac wyneb cyfarwydd ar y cyfryngau. Fe'i ganwyd yn Nhre-boeth, Abertawe, a bu'n byw am ddegawd yn Nhre-saith cyn symud i Nefyn.

Anwen Pierce
Fe'i magwyd yn Llandysul, ond erbyn hyn mae hi wedi ymgartrefu ym mhentref Bow Street ac yn olygydd i'r Cyngor Llyfrau. Mae hi'n aelod o dîm Tal-y-bont ar *Y Talwrn*.

Dafydd John Pritchard
Brodor o Nant Peris sy'n byw bellach yn Llanbadarn Fawr, ger Aberystwyth. Ef yw Rheolwr Mynediad at Gasgliadau Llyfrgell Genedlaethol Cymru. Enillodd Goron Eisteddfod Genedlaethol Cymru yn 1996.

John Roderick Rees
Ar ôl cyfnod fel athro Cymraeg yn Ysgol Uwchradd Tregaron, bu, fel ei dad a'i daid, yn magu cobiau Cymreig ar y tyddyn teuluol ym Mhenuwch. Enillodd y Goron genedlaethol yn 1984 ac 1985. Bu farw yn 2009.

Manon Rhys
Llenor a bardd o Gwm Rhondda ond sydd bellach yn byw yng Nghaerdydd. Mae ganddi gysylltiadau teuluol cryf gyda Cheredigion ac mae wedi ennill y Fedal Ryddiaith a'r Goron genedlaethol.

Geraint Roberts
Brodor o Lanfarian, ger Aberystwyth. Ymsefydlodd yn ardal Caerfyrddin a bu'n Bennaeth Ysgol Gyfun y Strade yn Llanelli. Mae'n enillydd cyson mewn eisteddfodau ac yn un o sylfaenwyr Ysgol Farddol Caerfyrddin.

Eurig Salisbury
Brodor o Langynog, sir Gaerfyrddin, sydd erbyn hyn yn byw yn Aberystwyth ac yn ddarlithydd yn Adran y Gymraeg ac Astudiaethau Celtaidd y Brifysgol. Enillodd y Fedal Ryddiaith yn Eisteddfod Genedlaethol Sir Fynwy yn 2016.

Iestyn Tyne
Bardd a cherddor sydd wedi ennill Cadair a Choron Eisteddfod Genedlaethol yr Urdd. Yn fab fferm o Foduan ym Mhenrhyn Llŷn, mae ar hyn o bryd yn byw yng Nghaernarfon ac yn dilyn ei waith fel cyfieithydd a golygydd.

Gair am y lluniau

Braint oedd derbyn y cynnig i gyflwyno ffotograffau i gyd-fynd â'r gyfrol hon. Roedd gen i eisoes storfa o luniau o Geredigion a fyddai'n ateb y galw ar gyfer rhai o'r cerddi i'r dim, ac roeddwn yn edrych ymlaen yn eiddgar at grwydro'r sir yn ystod y gwanwyn i dynnu rhagor.

Ni wyddwn bryd hynny fod newid byd ar ein gorwel. Fe ddaeth y pandemig â bywyd arferol i stop, a doedd crwydro'n hamddenol ddim bellach yn ddoeth nac ychwaith, ar adegau, yn gyfreithiol bosib. Roedd yn rhaid gwneud y gorau o'r sefyllfa, a thynnu'r lluniau newydd o fewn terfynau'r cyfyngiadau annisgwyl.

Mae rhai cerddi yn gofyn am ddehongliad lled lythrennol, tra mae eraill yn caniatáu – weithiau'n gorfodi – creu ymateb gweledol mwy amwys. Nid yw pob llun a geir yma felly'n gaeth, megis cerdyn post, i union leoliad manwl na chyfnod penodol ambell gerdd.

Wynebwyd ambell gyfyng-gyngor nad oedd a wnelo dim â thymor na hawl i deithio, nac ystyr nac ysbryd cerdd, e.e. beth a wnawn efo'r rheilffordd rhwng Aberystwyth a Chaerfyrddin, sydd ddim yn bod bellach – ai dangos yr hyn sydd wedi esblygu lle roedd y trac (sef llwybr cerdded a beicio), neu geisio dal ysbryd y lein drwy ddangos traciau sy'n bodoli mewn man arall? Ar daith pererin, a ddylwn ddangos y mannau hynny sydd yn britho'r daith, neu geisio dangos baich corfforol neu ysbrydol y pererin? Pan mae rhod y gerdd wedi troi, a'r byd a ddisgrifir ynddi wedi darfod, a ddylwn rywsut ffugio'r golud a fu, ynteu gofnodi'r dadfeiliad? Materion megis y rhain sy'n poeni dychymyg y ffotograffydd hwn yn ystod yn nos!

Does ond gobeithio y bydd y darllenydd yn derbyn cystal mwynhad o'r lluniau ag a gefais innau o'u tynnu, eu dethol a cheisio'u cyplysu â'r cerddi.

Hoffwn eilio'r diolchiadau sydd gan Idris Reynolds ar flaen y gyfrol, gan ategu fy niolch innau iddo fo ac i bawb arall a hwylusodd y ffordd, yn arbennig deulu hynaws Caffi'r Emlyn, Euros Lewis, Naphtali (y crydd) ac wrth gwrs Marian, a droediodd y llwybrau oll gyda mi.

Iestyn Hughes

Cydnabyddiaethau

Alan Llwyd, *Yr Ail Gasgliad Cyflawn* (Cyhoeddiadau Barddas, 2015), 356.

Aneirin Karadog, *Bylchau* (Cyhoeddiadau Barddas, 2016), 12.

Ceri Wyn Jones (gol.), *Cerddi Dic yr Hendre* (Gwasg Gomer, 2010), 156.

Ceri Wyn Jones (gol.), *Pigion y Talwrn 12* (Cyhoeddiadau Barddas, 2017), 126–7.

Ceri Wyn Jones, *Dauwynebog* (Gwasg Gomer, 2007), 66–7.

Cyril Jones, *Eco'r Gweld* (Cyhoeddiadau Barddas, 2012), 91.

D. Islwyn Edwards (gol.), *Cerddi W. J. Gruffydd* (Gwasg Gwynedd, 1990), 20–1.

Dafydd John Pritchard, *Lôn Fain* (Cyhoeddiadau Barddas, 2013), 74.

Dai Rees Davies, *Y Dwys a'r Digri* (Cyhoeddiadau Barddas, 2007), 25.

Dewi Pws, *Popeth Pws* (Y Lolfa, 2015), 108.

Donald Evans, *O'r Bannau Duon* (Cyhoeddiadau Barddas, 1987), 74.

Emyr Oernant, *Tan-y-groes Tan Greisis* (Aberteifi).

Eurig Salisbury, *Llyfr Glas Eurig* (Cyhoeddiadau Barddas, 2008), 18–19.

Gwyneth Lewis, *Tair Mewn Un* (Cyhoeddiadau Barddas, 2005), 125.

Geraint Roberts, *Desg Lydan* (Cyhoeddiadau Barddas, 2020), 20.

Gwenallt Llwyd Ifan, *DNA* (Cyhoeddiadau Barddas, 2021), 8-9.

Huw Meirion Edwards, *Lygad yn Llygad* (Gwasg y Bwthyn, 2013), 17–18.

Hywel Griffiths, *Llif Coch Awst* (Cyhoeddiadau Barddas, 2017), 11.

Idris Reynolds (gol.), *I Gofio'r Gaeafau: Cynnyrch Dosbarth Barddol Llambed* (Aberteifi, 2018).

Iestyn Tyne, *Ar Adain* (Cyhoeddiadau'r Stamp, 2018), 11 a 45.

Islwyn Edwards, *O'r Pren i'r Pridd* (Gwasg Gwynedd, 1986), 24.

Iwan Llwyd a Myrddin ap Dafydd (goln.), *Cywyddau Cyhoeddus* (Gwasg Carreg Gwalch, 1994), 21.

Iwan Llwyd, *Be 'Di Blwyddyn Rhwng Ffrindia?* (Gwasg Taf, 2003), 35.

John Roderick Rees, *Cerddi Newydd 1983–1991* (Cyhoeddiadau Barddas, 1992), 11.

Lyn Ebenezer, *Cerddi'r Bont* (Gwasg Carreg Gwalch, 2011), 22.

Manon Rhys, *Stafell fy Haul* (Cyhoeddiadau Barddas, 2018), 83–4.

Menna Elfyn, *Mynd Lawr i'r Nefoedd* (Gwasg Gomer, 1986), 19.

Myrddin ap Dafydd, *Pen Draw'r Tir* (Gwasg Carreg Gwalch, 1998), 9.

Richard Jones, *Garej Paradwys* (Gwasg Carreg Gwalch, 2019), 122.

T. Llew Jones, *Y Fro Eithinog* (Gwasg Gomer, 2015), 225, 233.

Tudur Hallam, *Parcio* (Cyhoeddiadau Barddas, 2019), 118–19.

Vernon Jones, *Gogerddan a Cherddi Eraill* (Gwasg Gomer, 1982), 37.

Ymddangosodd rhai o'r cerddi hefyd yn *Taliesin*, *Barddas*, *Cyfansoddiadau a Beirniadaethau Eisteddfod Genedlaethol Caerdydd a'r Fro 2018*, ac ar raglen *Y Talwrn*, BBC Radio Cymru.

G000048725

CHELSEA
FOOTBALL CLUB
PREMIER LEAGUE
Champions
2016/17

CHELSEA
FOOTBALL CLUB
PREMIER LEAGUE
Champions
2016/17

Production Editor: Harri Aston
Photography: Darren Walsh, Getty Images, PA Images
Writers: David Antill, Richard Godden, Dominic Bliss, James Sugrue
Design: Ben Renshaw, Glen Hind, Colin Harrison
Cover design: Colin Harrison
Sub-editor: Simon Monk
Statistics: Paul Dutton
Thanks to: Andy Jones, Kevin Newman

First published in Great Britain and Ireland in 2017 by
Trinity Mirror Sport Media, PO Box 48, Old Hall Street, Liverpool, L69 3EB.

www.tmsportmedia.com
@SportMediaTM

1

Hardback ISBN: 9781910335758
eBook ISBN: 9781911613091

Printed by KINT Ljubljana

CONTENTS

TERRY
26

HAYS
YOKOHAMA
TYRES
10

30

COUR OIS
13

Working his magic

When Antonio Conte arrived at Chelsea Football Club in the summer of 2016, Blues fans had plenty of reason for optimism about what the Italian could bring to SW6, but how many could honestly say they foresaw exactly how much of a success his first season in English football would be?

His reputation preceded him: a serial winner as both a player and a manager, his spell in charge of Italy came to an unlucky end on penalties against Germany at the quarter-final stage of last year's European Championship, where any Blues fans who were not overly aware of the man who had accumulated a glittering array of honours in Serie A suddenly became familiar with his undoubted ability as a coach.

However, he arrived at a club whose 10th place finish in the 2015/16 campaign represented our worst top-flight performance in two decades. Even the most ambitious of supporters would have been hard pushed to imagine what was to come, but Conte's vision – based predominantly around everybody giving him every ounce of effort they possibly could – was clear from the outset.

"The most important thing for us must be the passion for football. If you haven't got that, it's no good. This concept is very important," he declared in his first few weeks at the helm. "I have always worked a lot – a lot! – both as a player and as a manager, and I think this is my real secret: great work and great passion for football.

"My work is very important for me. I love to fight for the victory, I love to win, and I try to do everything I can to reach my target. I think if you want to reach success, it's important to put yourself into your work. I ask 110 per cent of myself and for this reason I demand that my players, my staff and all the people who work with me give me 110 per cent as well.

"I'm a person that wants to win, that works very hard to reach victory. It's important for me because when I achieve the win, I reach peace in my mind. I know I change my attitude and my behaviour

ANTONIO CONTE

during the game because I love to play the game together with my players. If we are winning, or if we are losing, I want them to see I am very close with them. I want them to see we are fighting for the win together."

They were certainly not empty words. Rarely, if ever, has a Chelsea manager showed such passion on the touchlines. From our very first match, at home to West Ham, Conte kicked every ball, threw himself into every challenge and celebrated every goal like a man possessed. It was impossible not to be carried along with his enthusiasm, and it was clear from the outset we were all going to love him.

A dramatic late win against the Hammers lit the touch paper for the Blues and Conte's exuberant behaviour – not to mention his joy for winning – fired

our souls. He emotionally thanked the fans for their support in his post-match press conference and a special bond was forged.

Three wins and a draw from our first four league fixtures provided a solid foundation, before back-to-back games against Liverpool and Arsenal provided the first opportunity to see how our head coach handled adversity. The answer, as we all know now, was emphatically, and it hinged on a formation switch which would prove so effective, one newspaper's season review hailed it as "arguably the most significant tactical decision in the Premier League's history."

A 2-1 home defeat against the Reds was followed by a first half to forget at the Emirates Stadium as the Blues trailed 3-0 at the interval. Something had to change and 10 minutes into the second period, Conte bravely switched to a three-man defence, employing Marcos Alonso and Cesar Azpilicueta as wing-backs. The game may have been lost in the opening period, but what he saw was enough to convince Conte to push forward with a system not too dissimilar to the one he had utilised while winning three consecutive Serie A titles with Juventus.

It was deployed from the start at Hull, only this time Azpilicueta moved into the three-man defence with what was to become the extremely familiar sight of Alonso and Victor Moses marauding up and down the flanks. The inclusion and subsequent importance

of the latter in our fortunes says as much as you need to know about Conte's managerial style as anything else. After signing for the club in 2012, Moses had struggled to force his way into a series of managers' plans on a consistent basis and had three loan spells away from Stamford Bridge. There are very few who could have predicted the impact he would have on our season, but Conte cares not for reputation, what has gone before or what other people think. His vision is clear and he has proven beyond all doubt that he knows exactly what to do in order to make his dreams a reality.

The Tigers were dispatched 2-0 and it was the start of a club record 13 straight league wins, which took

ANTONIO CONTE

us from the start of October all the way to the end of the year. The sequence propelled us to the top of the table and, quite rightly, saw Conte become the first person to win three consecutive Premier League Manager of the Month honours.

Among the many reflections on our glorious campaign, Conte was able to pinpoint the switch to three at the back as integral to what we achieved.

"This change was very important because we found the right balance and every single player enjoyed this type of situation," he said.

"It was the key moment for us and then a lot of work. I must be pleased because I found the players

who had never played this system and to change totally – a back three is very different to a back four – it was not easy. I found fantastic players and great men."

The new year brought about a temporary setback, as we lost at Tottenham, but the response was rapid as we kicked off our FA Cup campaign with a routine win over Peterborough. Brentford and Wolves were overcome before a mouth-watering quarter-final clash with Manchester United. For the press, it was the ideal opportunity to try to lead Conte into a negative comment about former Blues boss José Mourinho. Instead, his pre-match talk epitomised

ANTONIO CONTE

the class of the man, another facet of his personality which has made him such a popular figure here.

"For sure, he is one of the best in the world,' said Conte. 'I think that José Mourinho wrote a good part of the history of Chelsea. He won a lot with the players and he did a great job here. It is important not to forget this and I have great respect for him because he is a winner and I like his winning mentality. For sure, I hope in the future to try to emulate his wins here."

A 1-0 victory took us to a semi-final meeting with Tottenham at Wembley, where Conte's willingness to make the big calls on the big occasion was evident. Eyebrows were raised as Diego Costa and Eden Hazard were named on the bench, but the Blues excelled and ran out 4-2 winners on a truly memorable day.

From that point on, we never looked back in the title race, winning our six remaining fixtures and reclaiming the title with two matches to spare –

and as the first side to achieve 30 Premier League victories in a 38-game season. For Conte, it was the ultimate end to a stunning league campaign and his pride in what his team had achieved was plain to see.

"This is for my players," he stated. "It is a great achievement because this is the hardest championship to win in the world, and I have to say thanks to the players for their commitment, their attitude and their passion, and their will to do something great this season. They fought for this, so this win is for the players.

"Every game I feel like I have played with them. I show my passion and my will, my desire to stay with my players in every moment of the game. This is me, this is how I am. In the present, in the past, I stay with my players in positive and negative situations. So we won this title together."

Nobody could argue that Conte was a fitting recipient of the Premier League Manager of the Season award. Sadly, a narrow defeat to Arsenal in the FA Cup final meant we did not make it a Double, but with Conte at the helm, we have a leader whose insatiable appetite to win means the future looks very bright indeed.

"I think we have just started to light the fire and you must always have this fire in your soul, in your heart and in your head," he said.

"We must have a winning mentality, because if you have that you want to continue to win every season. It is not easy because in English football there are many, many teams that want to do the same things. We have to continue to work very hard and be stronger to try to repeat a good season."

Premier League

26

JOHN TERRY

It still seems strange to think that 2016/17 was John Terry's last season in a Chelsea shirt. Such was his impact over 22 incredible years at Stamford Bridge, it is hard to imagine the club without him.

However, it was a fitting farewell that the Blues' most successful player of all-time should depart as a Premier League champion, having hoisted the trophy into the air after his final appearance for the club against Sunderland.

It was an emotional occasion throughout the day as Terry ran out as Chelsea captain at the Bridge for the last time, playing the first 26 minutes before his team-mates lined up to show their appreciation for our No26 as he was replaced by Gary Cahill.

JT was still setting records in his last season here, too, not least becoming the first person to skipper five title-winning sides in the Premier League, having already led us to glory in 2005, 2006, 2010 and 2015. He may have featured less on the field in 2016/17 but Terry played as big a part as ever in the changing room and on the training pitch.

Showing the same professionalism which has served both him and Chelsea so well ever since he broke into the first-team as a 17-year-old, Terry was a key figure in galvanising the players into a solid unit under Antonio Conte. This was demonstrated by the frequency with which our first-team head coach thanked his captain for his immeasurable help during Conte's debut campaign in English football.

As sad as it may be that Terry will never take to the Stamford Bridge pitch in a Chelsea shirt again, it was only right that he bow out the same way he played – as a captain, leader, legend and champion.

JOHN TERRY
26
PROPER CHELS
JT
THANK YOU FOR EVERYTHING
26
FOOTBALL CLUB
YOKOHAMA
TYRES
26

YOKOHAMA
TYRES

“I can’t tell you how happy I am to be going out at the Bridge with a title celebration. I could not have asked for more after 22 incredible years at this great club.”

Premier League
Premier
Champ
CHAMP
YOKOHAMA TYRES

ZOUMA
5
YOKOHAMA TYRES

CONTE SAYS...

"This season I have seen what an important figure he is here, he has helped me a lot and with his work, day by day, he is the best possible example to every other player."

STATS...

John Terry's only goal of the season, against Watford in our penultimate Premier League fixture, saw him extend his own record by scoring in that competition for the 17th consecutive campaign, dating back to 2000/01. No other defender comes anywhere near that incredible run, with the next best being 10 straight seasons, set by Liverpool's Sami Hyypia and matched by our own Gary Cahill in 2016/17. Only seven more to go, Gaz!

JOHN TERRY	
Position: Defender	
Date of birth: 07.12.80	
Place of birth: Barking	
2016/17 PREMIER LEAGUE	
Appearances	6+3
Minutes	536
Goals	1
Assists	0

Assists are judged not for the last touch but by the subjective view of the club statistician for a crucial part played in the goal. Minutes include stoppage time.

Premier League
Premier League
Premier League
Premier League
Premier League
adizero

11

PEDRO

There were signs at the end of his first season at the club, in 2015/16, that Pedro had acclimatised to life in the Premier League, with a strong conclusion to the campaign helping him to finish as our third-highest scorer.

Those who had prematurely written off the Spaniard were perhaps not fully aware of the quite staggering haul of major honours he had accrued with Barcelona by the time he joined the Blues at the age of 28. He won multiple Champions League trophies with Barcelona, including scoring in the final, and a multitude of domestic honours – and that doesn't even take into account the World Cup and European Championship double he achieved with the Spanish national side.

This talented two-footed winger thrived in a more central role under Antonio Conte and his season burst into life when he scored our fastest goal of the Premier League season when netting after 30 seconds of the 4-0 win over Manchester United. It was a fine way to mark his 50th Chelsea appearance and his superlative form earned him a regular spot in the side ahead of Willian, who had won both Player of the Year awards in the previous campaign.

He also excelled as a wing-back on either flank during the early part of our FA Cup run, which coincided with a spell of five goals in six games at the turn of the year. There was never any question about his composure in front of goal, but he seems to be getting into the opposition penalty area more often in his slightly more central role in the 3-4-2-1 favoured by Conte.

None of this has happened by chance, for Pedro's dedicated approach to his trade is an example for everyone. He manages to combine hard work, humility and flair in one lethal package and all of it is underpinned by enormous talent. He is a coach's dream, but also a spectator's, and he plays with a smile on his face too.

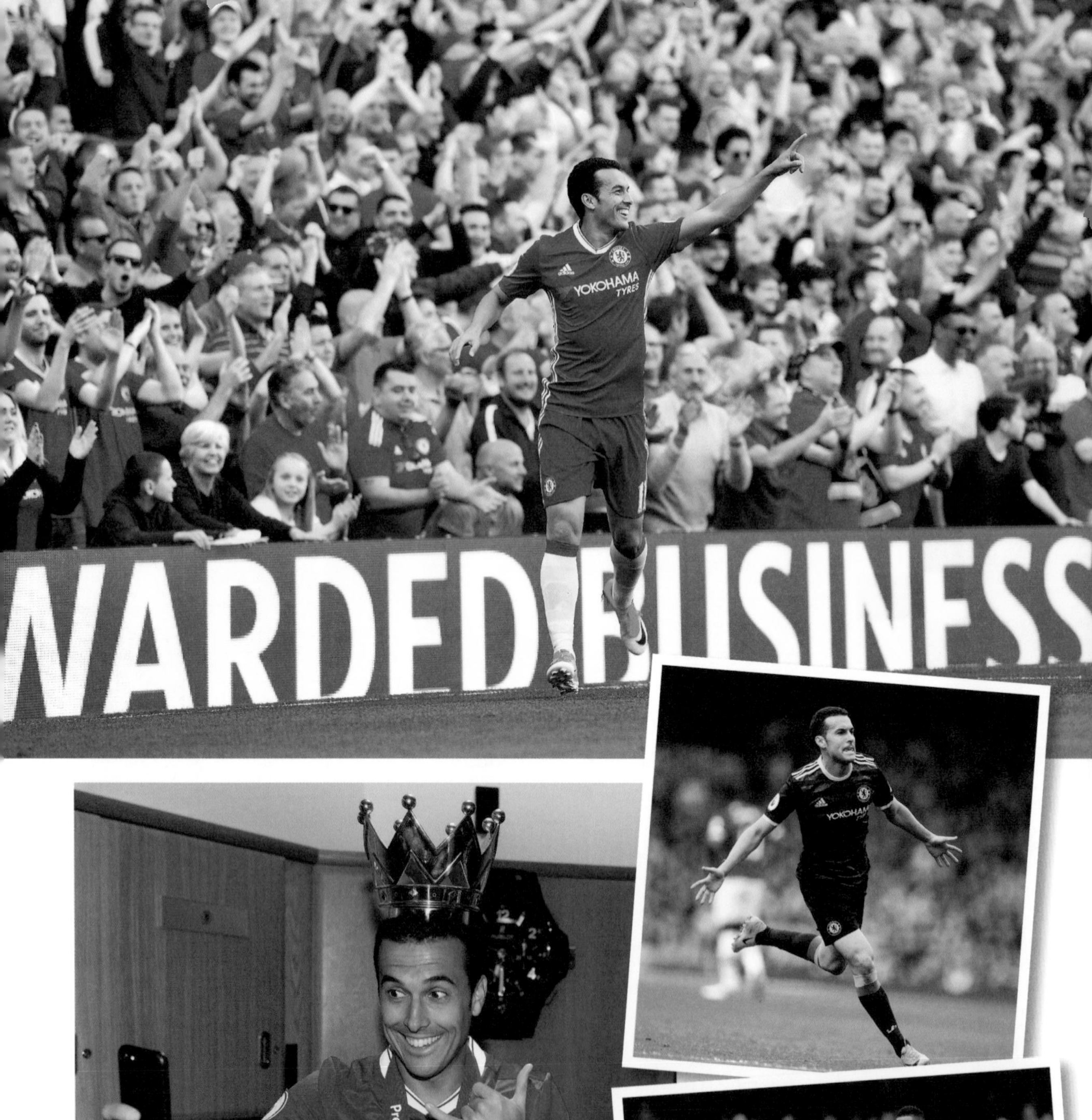
YOKOHAMA
TYRES
WARDED BUSINESS

bet365
YOKOHAMA
TYRES
17
19

"I understand the Premier League more now. It's very different compared to Spain – it's quicker, more intense, more competitive. I have to run a lot, play harder and I'm very quick, which helps me in the games here in England. There are more crosses into the box, and everything happens very quickly, which is good for the players and the spectators."

Sure
Sure
Sure
Sure

CONTE SAYS...

"He's a great player in the same way as Willian or Hazard or Diego Costa. I hope he continues in this way with this commitment, but Pedro has always had this quality. Now the formation is exploiting his characteristics better than before."

STATS...

One Goal of the Month award-winning strike across the course of a campaign is impressive enough, but to have two to your name takes some going. That's exactly what Pedro did, with his strike against Spurs in November followed up with a prize-winning effort at Goodison Park in our win over Everton in April. Even more impressive was the fact he scored the first with his right foot and the second with his left.

PEDRO	
Position: Midfielder	
Date of birth: 28.07.87	
Place of birth: Santa Cruz de Tenerife, Spain	
2016/17 PREMIER LEAGUE	
Appearances	26+9
Minutes	2262
Goals	9
Assists	13

adidas
Premier League

10

EDEN HAZARD

For the third season in four, Eden Hazard finished the campaign as Chelsea's Player of the Year, becoming just the second man to complete the hat-trick after Frank Lampard.

It is not difficult to see why Blues fans have taken the brilliant Belgian to their hearts, for his outlook on and off the pitch is quite simple. Nothing is overcomplicated, everything is positive and he tries to enjoy himself. Every time the ball arrives at his feet, he is already mapping out a route to goal, and he has the nous and trickery to make it look easy.

Having finished 2015/16 in fine form, Hazard netted our first goal against West Ham but his season, like that of so many of his team-mates, truly exploded into life once Antonio Conte changed the shape of his side at the start of October.

The benefit could be seen when he scored in three consecutive Premier League games for the first time, resulting in him being voted PFA Fans' Premier League best player. He was also named Premier League Player of the Month for the first time, which is quite remarkable considering his consistent excellence over the past five years.

He made his 150th Premier League appearance away at Middlesbrough in November 2016 and on Boxing Day at home to Bournemouth, from the penalty spot, netted his 50th Chelsea goal.

However, it was goal number 51 which was perhaps his best ever for the Blues. Receiving the ball in the centre-circle, he shrugged off Francis Coquelin and weaved in and out of the web spun by two Gunners centre-halves before lifting the ball over Petr Cech. It was awarded Premier League Goal of the Month for February and claimed him a second straight Chelsea Goal of the Season award.

Manchester City were perhaps the side to see the best of Hazard, as he scored three of our five goals against them, including both in the 2-1 home win in April. When the big games came around, the brilliant Belgian was, more often than not, decisive.

Premier League
HAMA
TYRES

#WILLIAMS40
JCB
WILLIAMS RACING

YOKOHAMA
TYRES

"I don't count how many goals I score, but I know because people talk a lot about that. I just want to win games – if we won 38 games but I scored zero goals I would be happy. I am not on the pitch thinking to score hat-trick, hat-trick, hat-trick – this is not me. I try to be the best in my style of play and if I can score it's good; if I score the winning goal it's better."

LOWTON
2
KEANE
15
HAZARD
10

YOKOHAMA
TYRES
CHELSEA
FOOTBALL CLUB
adidas

CONTE SAYS...

"My opinion of Eden is he's a great player. He has great talent. This season he improved a lot, not only on the pitch but also, I think, he's becoming stronger. Mentally stronger. At this level it's very important to try to have this step because it brings you up to the same level as the best players in the world. And Eden is starting to take this step. I see a player with good maturity, a player who wants to be decisive during the game."

STATS...

Hazard enjoyed his most prolific campaign in the Premier League as he netted 16 times in the competition, which surpassed his previous best of 14 which was set in both 2013/14 and 2014/15. He netted 12 times with his right foot – two of which were successfully converted penalties – and four with his left. This campaign was also the fourth out of five in which he has been directly involved in – either scoring or assisting – 20 goals or more.

EDEN HAZARD	
Position: Midfielder	
Date of birth: 07.01.91	
Place of birth: La Louviere, Belgium	
2016/17 PREMIER LEAGUE	
Appearances	36
Minutes	3119
Goals	16
Assists	15

Premier League

15

VICTOR MOSES

Chelsea's 2016/17 season provided plenty of good news stories and surprising revelations, but few could rival the emergence of Victor Moses as a first-choice wing-back.

Following a series of loan spells elsewhere in the Premier League, Moses was determined to prove that he was befitting of a role at Chelsea. He clearly made a good first impression on Antonio Conte, with our Italian boss informing the Nigerian international early on in pre-season he wanted him to remain with the Blues this campaign and foresaw an important part for him to play for the team.

How right Conte was, even if his impact on the pitch took a little longer to arrive. Like much that was good about the Blues' season, we first saw how effective Moses would be when we switched to a 3-4-2-1 system, our No15 taking the unfamiliar wing-back role on the right side. He had never played there before, but you would never have known, such was the assertive way he took to the position right from the start against Hull.

His performances in the next few months saw him rewarded with a two-year extension to his contract, keeping him at Stamford Bridge until 2021, and he also played a key role in our club-record run of 13 consecutive Premier League victories.

On top of the obvious contribution of his accomplished performances on the right, with his pace, stamina and physical strength all on constant display, he also kept the run going with his second-half winner against Tottenham in November, completing our comeback from going a goal behind early on to our London rivals. It didn't do his popularity with the Blues supporters any harm either!

adidas
YOKOHAMA
TYRES

Premier League

YOKOHAMA
adidas
Standard Chartered
BETEAST
CHELSEA SUPPORT

“Last year was one of the best years for me in my career and I’m delighted with that, and it’s thanks to the manager who gave me the opportunity to go out there and express myself.”

YOKOHAMA
TYRES
HTY
OFFICIAL
Carabao

CONTE SAYS...

"When I decided to change the system, I wanted to try him in this role, to work with him in a different situation, and he showed me great commitment to understand and to study the new role, above all in defensive situations. Now we have a complete player, offensively and defensively."

STATS...

Having not started any of our Premier League games before the switch to a back three in October, Victor Moses was picked in Antonio Conte's line-up for the next 22 consecutive matches in that competition. That run began with the first game with the new system at Hull City and only ended when injury prevented him from facing his first club Crystal Palace in April.

VICTOR MOSES	
Position: Wing-back	
Date of birth: 12.12.90	
Place of birth: Kaduna, Nigeria	
2016/17 PREMIER LEAGUE	
Appearances	29+5
Minutes	2603
Goals	3
Assists	4

Premier League
FOOTBALL CLUB
TYRES

CESC FABREGAS

He may have played fewer minutes on the pitch than in his previous two campaigns with Chelsea, but Cesc Fàbregas made every single one count and had arguably just as big an impact on our pursuit of the Premier League trophy as he did in our previous title triumph in 2014/15.

It is no surprise that the Spaniard's team-mates and manager Antonio Conte repeatedly praised his attitude and professionalism. For a player of Fàbregas' stature, the realisation that he was behind N'Golo Kanté and Nemanja Matic in Conte's plans at the start of the season must have been tough, but he showed great maturity to focus his energies on showing the manager what he could offer the team.

Even in the early stages of the campaign, he remained a key figure in the Chelsea dressing room, encouraging and cajoling his team-mates to achieve more. His effectiveness as a game-changing impact substitute was undoubted, frequently coming off the bench to use his passing ability and vision to turn defences as we chased a goal, or to control the tempo as we held on to a lead.

As the season went on he exerted more and more influence on the pitch, and when Matic suffered an injury at the start of December, Fàbregas seized the opportunity to impress. After coming into the line-up at Manchester City and setting up Diego Costa for our crucial second-half equaliser, as we went on to win 3-1 and assert our dominance in the title race, he then scored the only goal of the game two weeks later as we avoided a potential banana skin at Sunderland.

Those performances saw him playing an increasing role in the second half of the season as Conte switched between Matic's physicality and Fàbregas' finesse, depending on our opponents. He played an especially important part as we closed in on the title in the latter stages of the season, with his two assists in a 3-0 victory over Middlesbrough at Stamford Bridge, in particular, bringing us within touching distance of glory.

adidas
YOKOHAMA
TYRES

YOKOHAMA
TYRES

YOKOHAMA
TYRES
25

BOYD
YOKOHAMA
TYRES

YOKOHAMA
MANSION
FABREGAS
4

“Every single game I feel special because of what the fans have given me here, because of their support and how they have welcomed me since day one.”

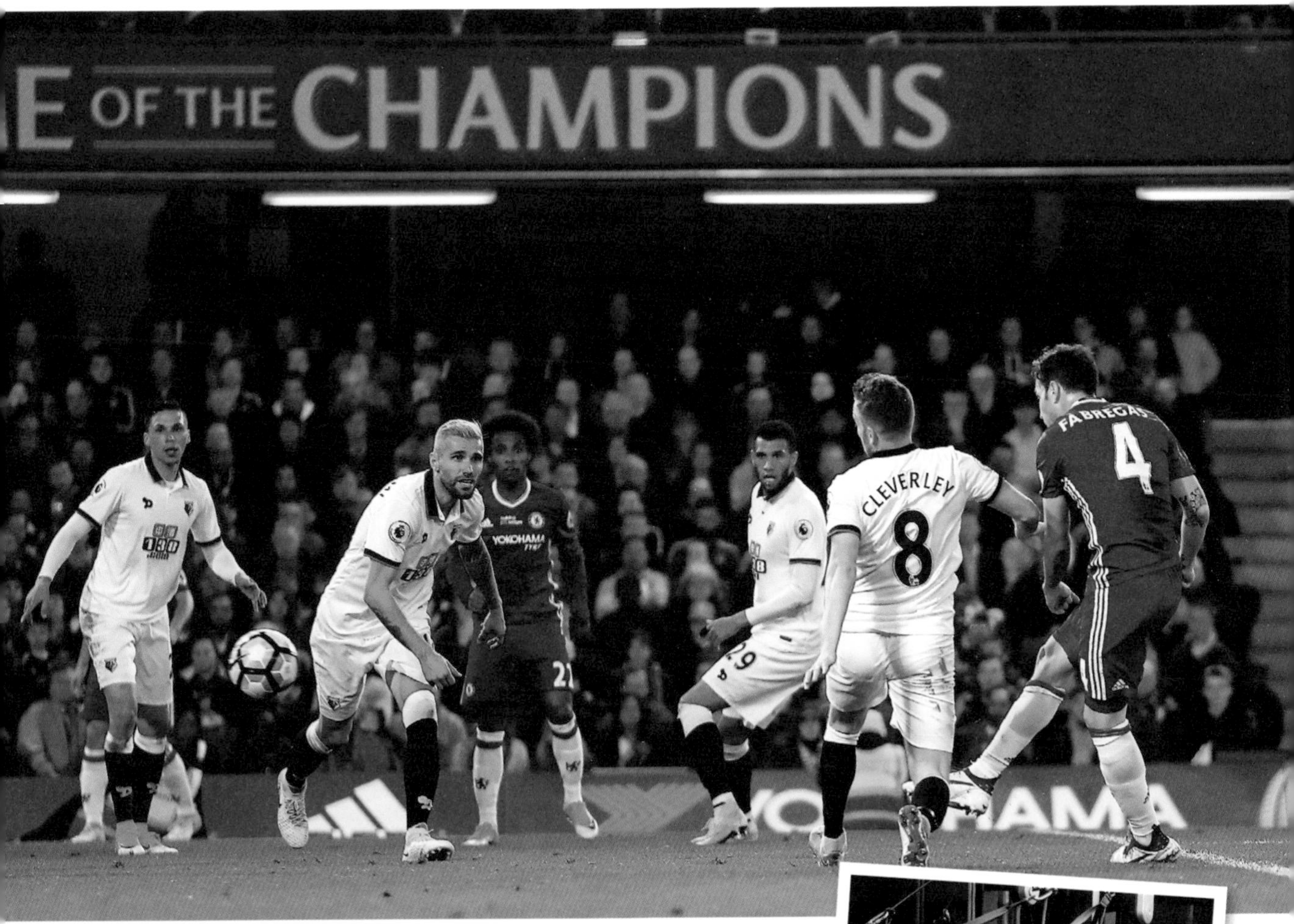
OF THE CHAMPIONS
FABREGAS
4
CLEVERLEY
8
YOKOHAMA

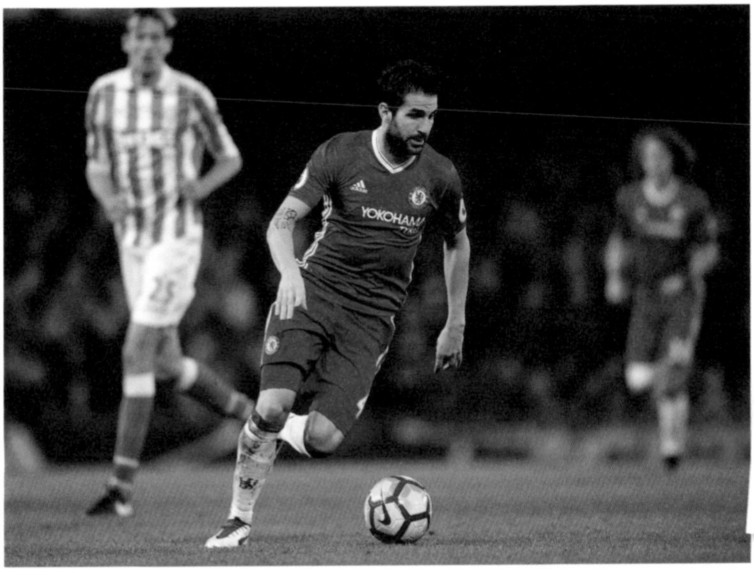
YOKOHAMA

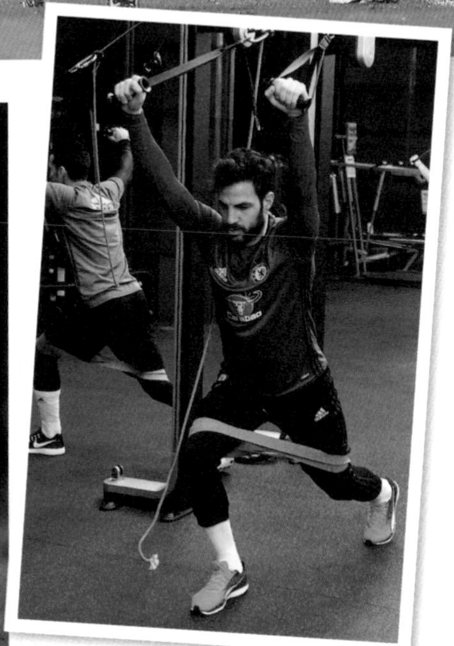

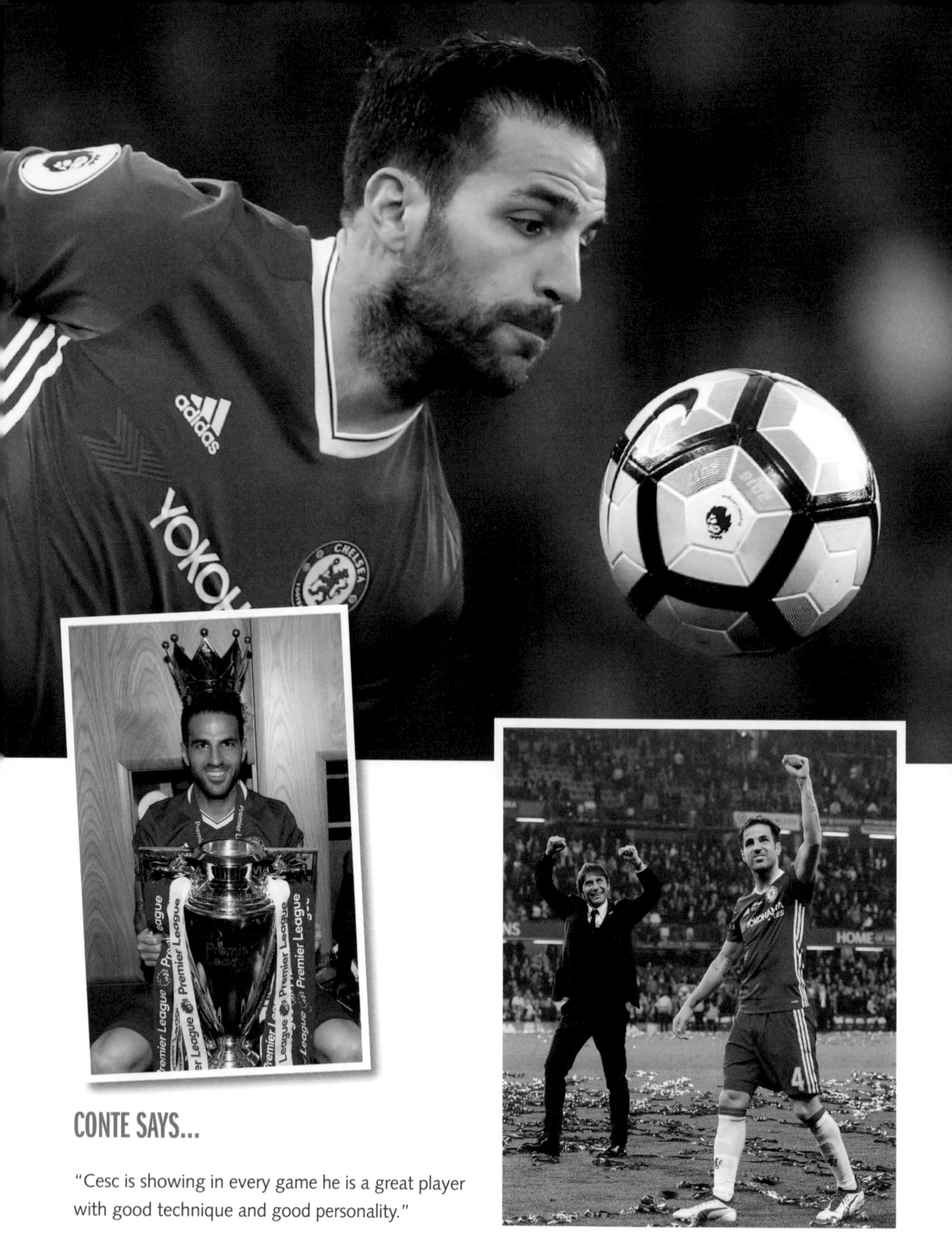

CONTE SAYS...

"Cesc is showing in every game he is a great player with good technique and good personality."

STATS...

Cesc Fàbregas is the first player to register 10 or more assists in six different Premier League seasons. He achieved that incredible record against Middlesbrough in May, when he set up Diego Costa for the opening goal and crossed into double figures for assists in 2016/17. Just for good measure, he also teed up Nemanja Matic later in the game to take his tally to 11.

CESC FABREGAS	
Position: Midfielder	
Date of birth: 04.05.87	
Place of birth: Arenys de Mar, Spain	
2016/17 PREMIER LEAGUE	
Appearances	13+16
Minutes	1457
Goals	5
Assists	14

Premier League
adidas
CHELSEA
FOOTBALL CLUB
YOKOHAMA
TYRES
Premier League
Golden Glove winner 2016/17

13

THIBAUT COURTOIS

When Thibaut Courtois kept a clean sheet against West Brom the day after his 25th birthday, it sealed his second Premier League title in three seasons as our first-choice shot-stopper to add to a remarkably impressive list of honours for the Belgian.

A fiercely competitive young man – something ingrained in him from an early age as the son of two volleyball players – Courtois has confirmed his status as one of the world's best goalkeepers.

With 16 clean sheets last term, he beat Tottenham's Hugo Lloris to the Premier League Golden Glove award. Ten of those came during our run of 13 league wins in the final three months of 2016, but they also returned in timely fashion at the end of April and beginning of May when Courtois was at his solid best as we kept out Everton, Middlesbrough and the Baggies.

The imposing Belgian's presence between the sticks means he can often make what seems impossible for other custodians appear decidedly simple. His positioning, awareness and concentration levels are the perfect attributes for the last line of defence, while his ability to stay focused, even in matches where he might not be called upon to do anything too dramatic, make him an ultra-reliable cog in Antonio Conte's well-oiled Chelsea machine.

On top of that, and perhaps most importantly, he is one of the finest shot-stoppers around, as he proved on numerous occasions last term.

In any triumphant season, there are moments which could easily have sent fortunes down another path were it not for a moment of brilliance from one individual. Such an instance occurred in our 1-0 win over Sunderland at the Stadium of Light, when Courtois produced a stunning last-ditch save from Patrick van Aanholt which left Black Cats boss David Moyes proclaiming he thought the ball was in before Courtois produced a strong right hand to miraculously turn it around the post.

SILVA
21

CHAMP
JT CAPTAIN
Premier League
YOKOHAMA
TYRES
Golden Glove winner 2016/17
COURTOIS
13

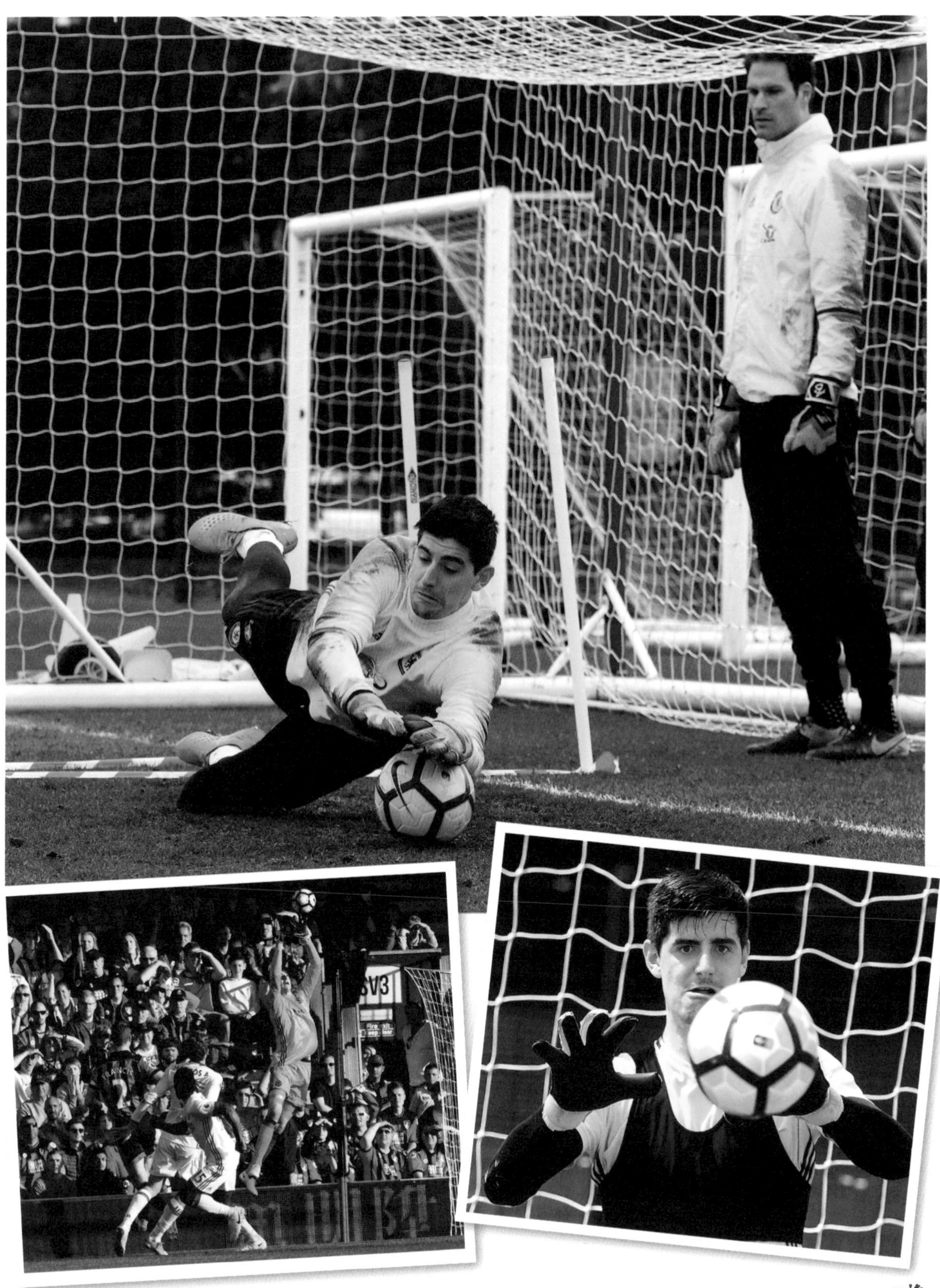

"The Premier League is very difficult to win, so to win it twice in three years is an amazing feeling. To win the Golden Glove in this division is very nice as well and I'm very proud of it. I have to thank all the team as well because you don't do it alone. Of course, there were key saves that kept a clean sheet, but the whole team defended well and it was a great year for everybody."

COURTOIS
0-1
dafabet
betway
bet

CONTE SAYS...

"For Thibaut it's more difficult because for the whole game you wait and you could lose concentration, but he is a fantastic goalkeeper. One of the best in the world, if not the best, and I'm pleased to have him in my team."

STATS...

In 2016/17 Courtois became only the second Chelsea goalkeeper to win the Premier League Golden Glove, following in the footsteps of Petr Cech, with his 16 clean sheets coming from 36 appearances. He made 68 saves across the course of the league campaign.

THIBAUT COURTOIS	
Position: Goalkeeper	
Date of birth: 11.05.92	
Place of birth: Bree, Belgium	
2016/17 PREMIER LEAGUE	
Appearances	36
Minutes	3448
Clean sheets	16

Premier League
TYRES

28

CESAR AZPILICUETA

Chelsea's 'Mr Reliable', who seems to adapt seamlessly to any new role handed to him. Having signed as a right-back in 2012, he has since shown himself to be a top-class left-back and last year he moved to a more central role, on the right side of Antonio Conte's back three.

Azpilicueta matches elegance with dynamism and is routinely praised by team-mates, fans and pundits alike for his remarkable work-rate. He simply doesn't believe in lost causes and his combination of intelligence, anticipation and pace make him a ruthless recoverer of possession.

His popularity with the supporters was almost instant, in part due to the good humour with which he greeted the chant they created for him upon his arrival. "Az-pi-li-cue-ta! We'll just call you Dave!"

Well, 'Dave' has now been an essential part of two Premier League winning sides, in two rather different roles. His intensity summed up the way this Chelsea side worked without possession throughout the campaign, breathing down opponents' necks and refusing to give them an inch in which to work. It is that kind of unheralded work, which he took to zealously from the beginning to the end of the season, which makes him the ultimate team player.

OME OF THE CHAMPIONS
SAFETY STEWARD
YOKOHAMA TYRES
adidas

Premier League

28
YOKOHAMA TYRES

6
28

"I've always been able to adapt to new positions and I think that made me better as a player. I've taken on every challenge in order to improve myself."

CHELSEA
FOOTBALL CLUB
HAMA

AZPILICUETA
28

YOKOHAMA
TYRES

CONTE SAYS...

"It was a massive season for him. He has played in a fantastic way and when you have this type of player it is great for the club. He is a model footballer and he can play in different roles. If I ask him to go and put on the gloves and to play in goal he is ready."

STATS...

Cesar Azpilicueta became only the fourth outfield player in Premier League history – after Gary Pallister, John Terry and Wes Morgan – to play every minute of every game in a title-winning campaign. In the penultimate game of the season, with the title secured three days previously, he showcased his versatility when he switched to right wing-back at home to Watford and got himself on the Premier League scorers' list for 2016/17 with a well-struck effort before half-time.

CESAR AZPILICUETA	
Position: Defender	
Date of birth: 28.08.89	
Place of birth: Pamplona, Spain	
2016/17 PREMIER LEAGUE	
Appearances	38
Minutes	3,642
Goals	1
Assists	6

CHELSEA
FOOTBALL CLUB
OKOHAMA
TYRES

Premier League

5

KURT ZOUMA

The 2016/17 season was always going to be one of recovery for Kurt Zouma after the Frenchman's breakthrough campaign had been cut short by a serious knee injury the previous January.

However, the obvious progress made in his return over the course of the past year showed plenty of signs he will be back competing for a regular spot in our defence with a full pre-season under his belt.

Despite still being in the early stages of that recovery, and therefore unable to train with the rest of the squad, Antonio Conte showed his desire to keep Zouma involved by taking the young centre-back on tour in pre-season, providing him with the perfect motivation during his lengthy absence.

His return to competitive action actually came with the Chelsea Under-23s, in our penalty shoot-out win over Oxford United's first team in the Checkatrade Trophy at Stamford Bridge in November, but he was back in the senior side for the start of our FA Cup campaign in early January.

Zouma had an important role to play in our run to that competition's final, playing the full 90 minutes of our first three matches as well as coming off the bench in the quarter-final win over Manchester United.

The last of those came after an important shift in the tone of his appearances, as he went from being given game time to improve his match fitness, to becoming an important tactical option for Conte.

The sight of Zouma replacing Victor Moses in the second half as we held on to a lead became increasingly common in the latter stages of 2016/17 when our Italian manager felt a more cautious approach was needed, slotting Zouma into the back three to allow Cesar Azpilicueta to take Moses' place at wing-back.

ZOUMA
5
23

Premier League
Premier League

YOKOHAMA
TYRES
CHEVROLET
6

HOM
Premier League

“It was tough because everybody loves playing football and I was out for a long time, but watching the boys doing so well was good and it helped the time to go quicker.”

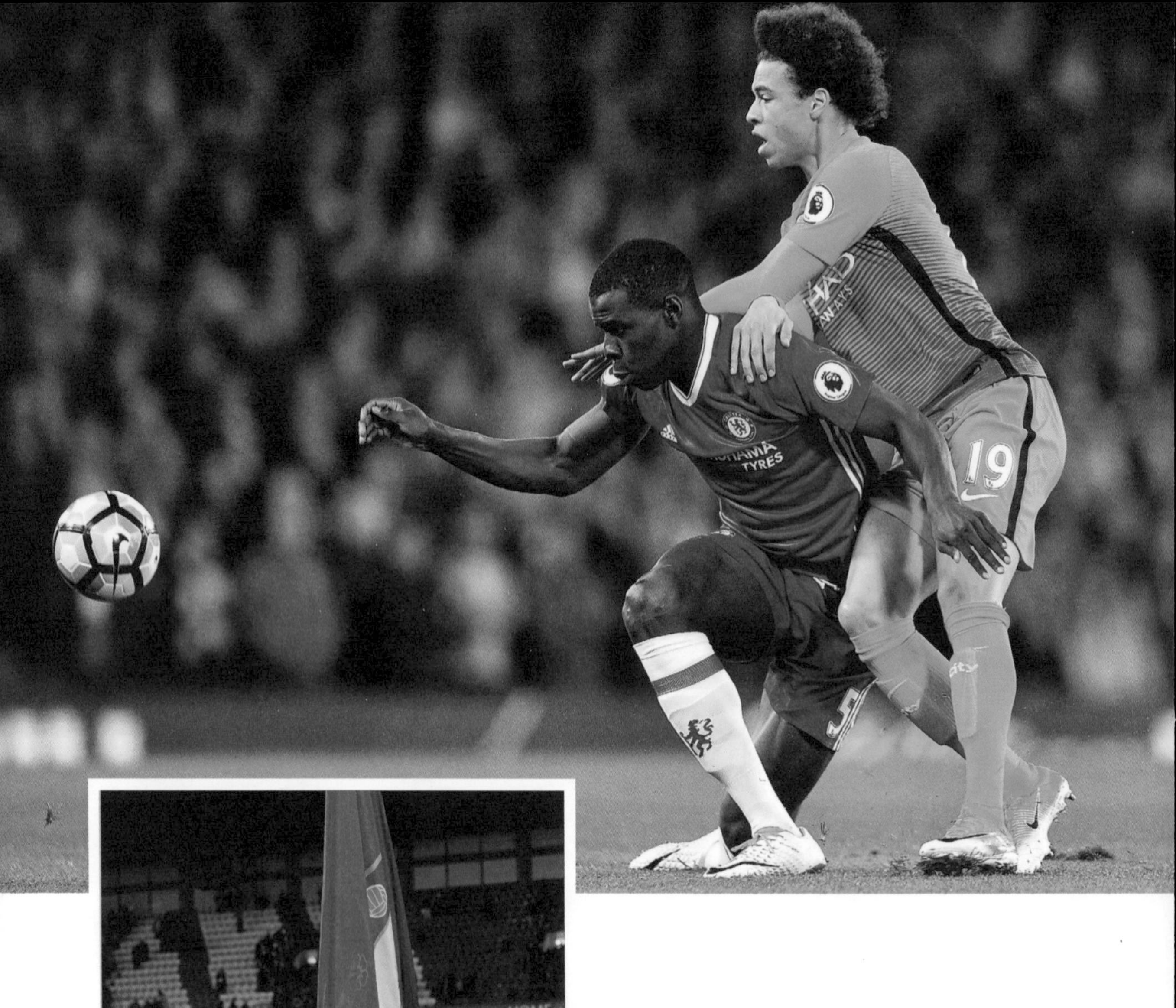

CONTE SAYS...

"I am very happy because he is fully recovered after a very bad injury so I can have another central defender and a good central defender, a young one with great potential. Now he is in good shape and he is ready to play and to restart his career. We know he can improve a lot."

STATS...

Kurt Zouma was one of the scorers during an epic 34-penalty shoot-out in 2016/17, which set a new record for the longest ever in English football. It came on his return to competitive action after nine months out injured, for our Under-23s against Oxford United in the Checkatrade Trophy, and the French defender played his part by scoring both his efforts from the spot en route to a 13-12 victory for the Blues.

KURT ZOUMA	
Position: Defender	
Date of birth: 27.10.94	
Place of birth: Lyon, France	
2016/17 PREMIER LEAGUE	
Appearances	3+6
Minutes	234
Goals	0
Assists	1

STORY OF THE SEASON

Diego Costa celebrates scoring our late winner against West Ham

RECLAIMING THE CROWN
STORY OF THE SEASON

MATCHDAY 1

Stamford Bridge, 16.08.16

CHELSEA 2 WEST HAM UNITED 1

Hazard 47 (pen), Diego Costa 89 · Collins 77

Chelsea's first competitive game under Antonio Conte saw a vibrant attacking display by the Blues which was rewarded with a fantastic late winner by Diego Costa.

The tempo was set from the very first minute, with the home side not allowing West Ham to settle on the ball.

With so much possession, chances eventually came. Branislav Ivanovic was close to catching out Adrian at his near post, while a trademark Eden Hazard curler was only just wide of the target.

The goal our performance merited was not long in coming after the interval, and it was Hazard who scored it. A clumsy challenge by Michail Antonio on Cesar Azpilicueta allowed the Belgian to smash home from the penalty spot.

West Ham looked to have stolen a point when James Collins scored late on, but Diego Costa had other ideas. Receiving the ball on the edge of the box, the Blues No 19 drove a low shot past Adrian. Stamford Bridge erupted, Conte celebrated with the fans and a new era had begun.

MATCHDAY 2

Vicarage Road, 20.08.16

WATFORD 1 CHELSEA 2

Capoue 55 · Batshuayi 80, Diego Costa 87

A brilliant late fightback, inspired by Antonio Conte's substitutions and sealed with a breakaway goal from Diego Costa, saw Chelsea maintain our 100 per cent start to the Premier League season.

The Blues lined up with 10 of the players who defeated West Ham last Monday, the only change an enforced one as an injury to Willian saw Pedro come into the starting XI.

The first goal arrived 10 minutes after the interval as Etienne Capoue volleyed past Thibaut Courtois.

With 20 minutes left, Conte introduced Victor Moses, Michy Batshuayi and Cesc Fàbregas over a seven-minute period – and the latter two were instrumental in turning the game around.

First, Batshuayi netted his first Blues goal with a close-range finish after Gomes parried Eden Hazard's shot. Then, with three minutes left, Fàbregas' sensational pass sent Diego Costa clear. The striker slipped the ball under the goalkeeper for his second late winner of the week.

Summer signing Michy Batshuayi opens his Blues account with the equaliser at Watford

138
.com

Victor Moses wheels away in celebration after scoring the third against Burnley

RECLAIMING THE CROWN
STORY OF THE SEASON

MATCHDAY 3

Stamford Bridge, 27.08.16
CHELSEA 3 BURNLEY 0
Hazard 9, Willian 41, Moses 89

The Blues made it three wins out of three in the Premier League with a dominant home victory over newly promoted Burnley.

The result never looked in doubt from the moment Eden Hazard broke the deadlock early on. The Belgian ace had started the season in fine form and this was something of a trademark goal as he drove at the Burnley rearguard before curling a superb right-footed shot past Tom Heaton.

There was no let up from the home side and although several chances went begging, our lead was doubled before the break courtesy of another excellent goal. Willian was the scorer on this occasion, bursting past Stephen Ward down the right and then firing his shot into the far corner.

Burnley rarely threatened the Blues' rearguard throughout the 90 minutes and the third goal our performance deserved came in the closing stages of the game. Two substitutes were involved as Pedro sent a teasing centre into the path of Victor Moses to make it 3-0.

MATCHDAY 4

Liberty Stadium, 11.09.16
SWANSEA CITY 2 CHELSEA 2
Sigurdsson 59 (pen), Fer 62 · Diego Costa 18, 81

Chelsea had to settle for a point against Swansea despite a strong performance in Wales, in a match which was lit up by a sparkling performance from Diego Costa.

The Spanish international opened the scoring in a first half we completely controlled, finishing instinctively from the edge of the penalty area after good work in the box by Oscar. However, we couldn't find a second before the break and were made to pay in the second half.

Firstly, Gylfi Sigurdsson equalised from the spot after Thibaut Courtois conceded a penalty. Then, just three minutes later, Leroy Fer gave the home side the lead with only their second shot on target, although there were certainly strong claims for a foul on Gary Cahill.

Thankfully Diego Costa struck again late on, saving the best until last. His spectacular overhead kick had too much power for defender Federico Fernandez to block after Branislav Ivanovic's shot was deflected up into the air. However, we couldn't find a winner during a frantic finish.

Diego Costa gives the Blues hope during the defeat against Liverpool at the Bridge

RECLAIMING THE CROWN
STORY OF THE SEASON

MATCHDAY 5

Stamford Bridge, 16.09.16

CHELSEA 1 LIVERPOOL 2

Diego Costa 61 · Lovren 17, Henderson 36

Diego Costa's second-half goal couldn't inspire a turnaround in Chelsea's fortunes as we slipped to our first defeat of the 2016/17 campaign.

Our first Friday night Premier League fixture in 14 years didn't begin as planned and we found ourselves trailing when Dejan Lovren was left unmarked at the back post to turn home an inviting cross from Philippe Coutinho.

If that goal could have been considered avoidable, the same could hardly be said of the second. There seemed to be little on when Jordan Henderson picked up the ball 30 yards from goal but he bent an unstoppable strike past Thibaut Courtois to double the Reds' advantage.

The response came on the hour when Diego Costa scored a goal which was beautifully crafted by Eden Hazard and Nemanja Matic, the latter showing quick feet and composure in the box to tee up the Blues No19 for a close-range finish.

However, we couldn't find a way through a stubborn defence and the points went back to Anfield with the visitors.

MATCHDAY 6

Emirates Stadium, 24.09.16

ARSENAL 3 CHELSEA 0

Sanchez 11, Walcott 14, Ozil 40

The Blues suffered a first Premier League defeat against Arsenal since October 2011 after three first-half goals secured the Gunners' victory at the Emirates Stadium.

Although both teams made a positive start to the game, it was the home side who took full advantage as they netted two goals in quick succession.

The first came as a result of a defensive lapse which allowed Alexis Sanchez a clear run at goal, the Chilean dinking the ball over Thibaut Courtois to punish the error.

However, it was a crisp passing move which teed up Theo Walcott for the second, which left us facing a huge task to get back into the match, and our hopes were dashed further when a Mesut Ozil sucker punch on the counter-attack made it 3-0 five minutes before the break.

Substitute Michy Batshuayi had our best chance of the game when a fine David Luiz pass from deep sent him scampering through on goal, but he was denied by Petr Cech and we suffered a second league defeat of the season.

Willian curls in the
opener against Hull City

RECLAIMING THE CROWN
STORY OF THE SEASON

MATCHDAY 7

KCOM Stadium, 01.10.16

HULL CITY 0 CHELSEA 2

Willian 61, Diego Costa 67

The Blues went into the international break on a high as Willian and Diego Costa both netted in the space of six second-half minutes to defeat the newly promoted Tigers.

The major talking point early on was Antonio Conte's decision to line up with a three-man defence, a system he utilised during his time in charge of both the Italian national team and Juventus.

Although we weren't able to create too many chances in the first half, after the interval it was a different story. First, Diego Costa went close when he rounded David Marshall and shot at goal, only to see his effort deflected on to the post before N'Golo Kanté fired over.

However, it proved to be a temporary reprieve for the Tigers as the Chelsea No19 won possession high up the pitch and fed Willian, who cut inside before curling an unstoppable effort into the far corner. Six minutes later, Diego Costa himself was on the scoresheet with an almost identical finish after Nemanja Matic's shot was deflected into his path.

MATCHDAY 8

Stamford Bridge, 15.10.16

CHELSEA 3 LEICESTER CITY 0

Diego Costa 7, Hazard 33, Moses 80

Chelsea ran out comfortable winners in a clash between the past two Premier League champions, moving to within three points of leaders Manchester City.

Diego Costa put the Blues ahead with his seventh goal of the season, reacting quickest to Nemanja Matic's flick-on from a corner to send a controlled left-footed volley past Kasper Schmeichel at the far post.

Our lead was extended just past the half-hour mark, owing to an improvised through-ball from Pedro and a smart finish by Eden Hazard. The Spaniard somehow volleyed the ball into his team-mate's path while on his back and Hazard rounded Schmeichel to finish into an empty net.

That goal came just after David Luiz had hit a post. While he would repeat the trick at the wrong end in the second half, in doing so he almost certainly denied Jamie Vardy a tap-in.

Victor Moses made the game safe with a tidy finish after being sent clear by a great flick from substitute Nathaniel Chalobah – a fitting end to an excellent performance.

Joyous scenes at the Bridge as N'Golo Kanté opens his Blues account against Manchester United

RECLAIMING THE CROWN
STORY OF THE SEASON

MATCHDAY 9

Stamford Bridge, 23.10.16

CHELSEA 4 MANCHESTER UNITED 0

Pedro 1, Cahill 21, Hazard 62, Kanté 70

Chelsea produced our finest display of the season to inflict Manchester United's biggest away defeat in the Premier League since a 5-0 drubbing at the Bridge in 1999.

On an emotionally-charged afternoon in west London as we celebrated the life of Matthew Harding on the 20th anniversary of his passing, the Blues put in a performance of which our former vice-chairman would have been proud.

A mix-up allowed Pedro to run through and round David De Gea after 30 seconds, and that lead was soon doubled by Gary Cahill from a corner. There was no surprise when the third goal went Chelsea's way, as Eden Hazard skipped inside Chris Smalling and slotted a precise finish past De Gea.

The icing on the cake came from N'Golo Kanté as he feinted past Smalling and beat De Gea. It was his first goal for the Blues and the delight on the faces of his team-mates and every supporter inside Stamford Bridge said it all.

MATCHDAY 10

St Mary's Stadium, 30.10.16

SOUTHAMPTON 0 CHELSEA 2

Hazard 6, Diego Costa 55

Eden Hazard and Diego Costa scored a goal in either half to hand the Blues a fourth consecutive Premier League victory with a clean sheet.

The Saints hadn't been beaten at home in eight months since our last visit to St Mary's, but they found themselves behind early on as Hazard netted for the third league game running for the first time in his Blues career.

The Belgian took a pass from Victor Moses in his stride and cut inside Steve Davis before drilling a left-footed shot through the legs of Fraser Forster.

Although the home side were seeing more of the ball, the better chances came our way and after Diego Costa was denied late in the first half by Forster, he made no mistake early in the second period.

His best work often occurs inside the box, but this time the Chelsea No19 displayed outstanding technique outside the area to fire home a rocket which took him back to the top of the Premier League scorers' chart.

CHELSEA
FOOTBALL CLUB
MANCHESTER
UNITED
CHEVROLET

Gary Cahill lashes home the second in the 4-0 triumph over Manchester United

Two Chelsea Pensioners lead the Blues out ahead of our match against Everton

RECLAIMING THE CROWN
STORY OF THE SEASON

MATCHDAY 11

Stamford Bridge, 05.10.16

CHELSEA 5 EVERTON 0

Hazard 19, 56, Alonso 20, Diego Costa 42, Pedro 65

There were fireworks in the sky and on the pitch on Bonfire Night as the Blues inflicted a five-goal drubbing of the Toffees with a clinical performance.

Eden Hazard put us ahead for the second week running with another of his trademark finishes, cutting in from the left onto his right foot and curling home a low effort.

There was a new name on the scoresheet when Marcos Alonso timed his run to perfection to crisply strike through the legs of Maarten Stekelenburg, and the Toffees keeper was equally helpless when Diego Costa lashed home Nemanja Matic's flick-on from a corner.

After the break, a wonderful move culminated in Hazard and Pedro exchanging passes before the Belgian finished at the near post. The scoring was complete when Pedro reacted quickest to the rebound following Hazard's shot.

MATCHDAY 12

Riverside Stadium, 20.10.16

MIDDLESBROUGH 0 CHELSEA 1

Diego Costa 41

Diego Costa's 10th Premier League goal of the season moved Chelsea to the top of the table as we won for the sixth straight game without conceding.

Middlesbrough had lost each of their previous six matches against us without finding the back of the net, so it always looked a tall order for the newly promoted side to get back into the game from the moment our No19 opened the scoring with a typically opportunistic finish.

Victor Valdes had already denied Pedro with a fine fingertip save, but there was little he could do to keep out Diego Costa's close-range effort shortly before the break.

It was an instinctive goal by the Spanish international, who reacted quickest to stab home the loose ball with his left foot when a corner kick was headed up in the air.

Marcos Alonso almost added a second shortly after the interval and Pedro went even closer when he hit the crossbar following another well-crafted move, but Boro offered little in attack as we moved a point clear at the top.

Eden Hazard (out of shot) opens the scoring in the Bonfire Night encounter with the Toffees

Pedro's magical curling effort levels the scores against Tottenham

RECLAIMING THE CROWN
STORY OF THE SEASON

MATCHDAY 13

Stamford Bridge, 26.11.16

CHELSEA 2 TOTTENHAM HOTSPUR 1

Pedro 45, Moses 51 · Eriksen 11

Conceding a first league goal in over 10 hours wasn't enough to prevent Chelsea making it seven top-flight wins on the spin after a fine comeback over our London rivals.

The Blues haven't been beaten by Spurs at Stamford Bridge since 1990, but that run looked to be under threat during a bright opening by the visitors which was rewarded with a goal when Christian Eriksen's fierce drive from outside the box swerved past Thibaut Courtois.

Although the Blues took time to get a foothold in the game, we were level by half-time thanks to an impressive strike by Pedro. Afforded far too much time and space on the edge of the box, the Spaniard curled home a sumptuous effort to score for the third consecutive home game.

The decisive strike wasn't long in arriving after the interval as Victor Moses netted yet another crucial goal. As Diego Costa drove into the box and fired a low cross through the area, Moses was left free to run into space and slot the ball past Hugo Lloris to ensure our fine run continued.

MATCHDAY 14

Etihad Stadium, 03.12.16

MANCHESTER CITY 1 CHELSEA 3

Cahill own goal 45 · Diego Costa 60, Willian 70, Hazard 90

The Blues moved clear at the top of the Premier League after producing a clinical counter-attacking display to come from a goal down and defeat Manchester City.

The home side led at the break through an unfortunate own goal by Gary Cahill, who diverted the ball past Thibaut Courtois from a Jesus Navas cross, but the game turned in the space of a few second-half minutes.

After Kevin De Bruyne smashed the crossbar, Chelsea equalised when Cesc Fàbregas pinged a sumptuous pass to Diego Costa, who fired past Claudio Bravo.

The striker then turned provider 10 minutes later, brilliantly outfoxing Nicolas Otamendi and sending an inch-perfect through-ball for Willian to run clear and finish.

Another breakaway goal in the last minute, this time by the electrifying Eden Hazard, settled the game before City lost their heads. Sergio Aguero was dismissed for a crude lunge on David Luiz, with Fernandinho also given his marching orders when he clashed with Fàbregas.

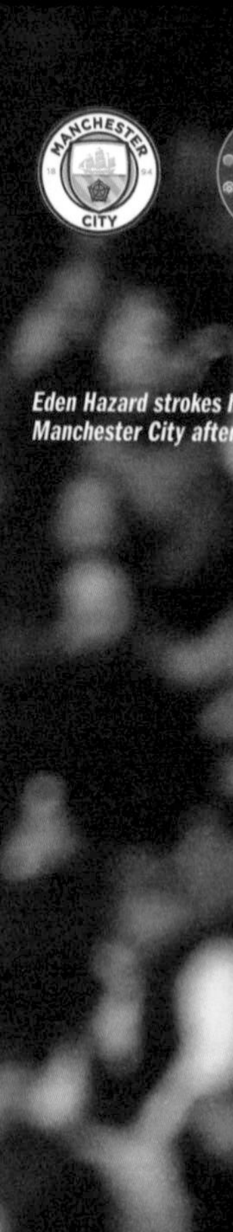

Eden Hazard strokes home the third against Manchester City after another clinical break

C.BRAVO
1

Cesc Fàbregas takes the plaudits after his goal that made the difference at Sunderland

RECLAIMING THE CROWN
STORY OF THE SEASON

MATCHDAY 15

Stamford Bridge, 11.12.16
CHELSEA 1 WEST BROMWICH ALBION 0
Diego Costa 76

Diego Costa scored a brilliant late winner which ensured West Bromwich Albion's long wait for a league win at Stamford Bridge continues.

The Baggies arrived in west London unbeaten in four matches and frustrated us for much of the game, with chances hard to come by for the in-form Blues. Indeed, our best opportunity of the opening half was Pedro's clever deflection from a low N'Golo Kanté shot which just missed the target.

Although West Brom kept plenty of men back at all times, the industrious Salomon Rondon posed an occasional threat – but Diego Costa displayed a perfect example of lone centre-forward play with his winning goal.

Chasing down a long ball by substitute Cesc Fàbregas, Chelsea's No19 robbed Gareth McAuley of possession wide on the right before cutting inside. With the angle against him, the stunning left-footed finish into the top far corner was befitting of a top-class striker.

MATCHDAY 16

Stadium of Light, 14.12.16
SUNDERLAND 0 CHELSEA 1
Fàbregas 40

A classy finish from Cesc Fàbregas separated Chelsea and Sunderland, but we were indebted to a pair of world-class saves by Thibaut Courtois as we recorded 10 Premier League wins in a row for only the third time.

Just as against West Brom, the Blues came up against a disciplined and well-organised rearguard designed to frustrate our attack, although on this occasion the breakthrough wasn't quite so long in the making. Fàbregas was the scorer, netting his first league goal of the season with a precise low finish from outside the box after being fed by Willian.

Jordan Pickford in the Sunderland goal had frustrated us until that moment and though he continued to make saves throughout, Courtois had to match him at the other end. As well as denying Adnan Januzaj on a breakaway, the Belgian made an even better save in the closing stages when he somehow kept out a goal-bound effort by former Blues defender Patrick van Aanholt.

Pedro's shot beats Artur Boruc to give Chelsea the lead against Bournemouth

RECLAIMING THE CROWN
STORY OF THE SEASON

MATCHDAY 17

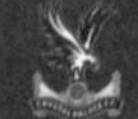 

Selhurst Park 17.12.16

CRYSTAL PALACE 0 CHELSEA 1

Diego Costa 43

The Blues equalled our club record of 11 consecutive league wins with a third 1-0 victory in the space of seven days.

Diego Costa was our match-winner with his 13th Premier League goal of the season coming shortly before the end of a scrappy first half which neither side was able to take by the scruff of the neck.

Antonio Conte's side were the only team not to have scored or conceded a headed goal this season, but that all changed when Cesar Azpilicueta advanced down the right and picked out our striker to nod us in front.

Although there was Palace pressure after the break, the best chances fell our way. N'Golo Kanté, Cesc Fàbregas and Marcos Alonso all tested the goalkeeper, while the latter also hit the underside of the bar with a free-kick.

The victory did come at a cost, however, as both Diego Costa and Kanté received yellow cards which ruled them out of the Bournemouth game.

MATCHDAY 18

Stamford Bridge, 26.12.16

CHELSEA 3 BOURNEMOUTH 0

Pedro 24, Hazard 49 (pen) · S Cook own goal 90+3

Chelsea set a new club record of 12 straight Premier League wins with a comfortable Boxing Day victory over Bournemouth.

The Blues were in control of the contest from the moment Pedro opened the scoring with another fine strike from distance, the Spaniard showing excellent composure to shift the ball from under his feet and loft a curling effort beyond the reach of Artur Boruc.

Our lead was doubled early in the second half when Eden Hazard converted a penalty after being felled by Simon Francis' clumsy challenge, becoming the sixth player to reach the 50-goal mark for the Blues in the Premier League.

Thibaut Courtois was made to work for his fourth consecutive clean sheet, with his save from substitute Benik Afobe perhaps his best of the afternoon, and the gloss was put on the victory in stoppage time when Pedro's jinking run finished with Steve Cook deflected the ball past his own keeper.

Diego Costa hammers home late on to
leave Stoke City beaten at the Bridge

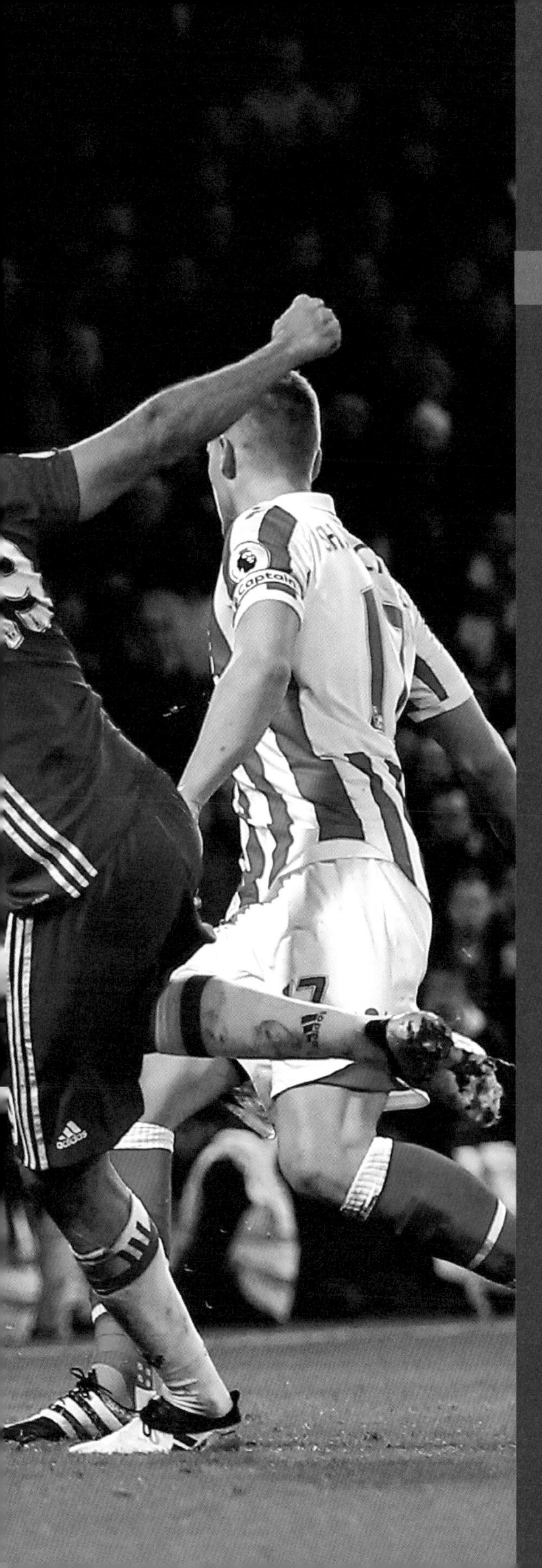

RECLAIMING THE CROWN
STORY OF THE SEASON

MATCHDAY 19

Stamford Bridge, 31.12.16

CHELSEA 4 STOKE CITY 2

Cahill 34, Willian 57, 65, Diego Costa 85 · Martins Indi 46, Crouch 64

The Blues closed out 2016 with a club-record 13th top-flight league win on the bounce, but we were made to work hard for the victory by a Stoke City side who equalised on two occasions in a thrilling second half.

Although Lee Grant made a number of excellent saves in the opening half-hour, there was no denying Gary Cahill the opening goal when the No24 rose highest to powerfully head home a corner by Cesc Fàbregas.

The Potters were level just a minute after the break through a smart finish by another centre-back, Bruno Martins Indi, but Willian soon fired the Blues back in front following a sublime lay-off by Eden Hazard from a Victor Moses cross.

Peter Crouch restored parity, but it was short lived as Willian was on target straight from the restart, Fàbregas again providing the assist. Victory was secured with five minutes remaining as Diego Costa doggedly held off two Stoke centre-halves before lashing home a sensational finish.

MATCHDAY 20

White Hart Lane, 04.01.17

TOTTENHAM HOTSPUR 2 CHELSEA 0

Alli 45+1, 54

Our club-record run of victories came to an end in north London after Dele Alli scored headers either side of half-time in a closely contested match decided by fine margins.

The Blues had a great chance to go ahead inside the first five minutes when Eden Hazard ran onto a clipped ball over the top and tried to catch Hugo Lloris off-guard by taking on the half-volley early, only to see his shot just miss the target.

It proved the best opportunity until first-half stoppage time, when Alli directed a header past Thibaut Courtois from Christian Eriksen's cross.

Our response after the interval was impressive, as Diego Costa forced a good save from Lloris and Hazard headed just wide, but Spurs took the wind out of our sails with another header by Alli, who was once again found by Eriksen.

The home side's defence stood firm as Antonio Conte tried to change our fortunes with a number of attacking changes, but a late David Luiz header which sailed over was our best opportunity.

Marcos Alonso celebrates with his team-mates after putting us two goals in front against Leicester

RECLAIMING THE CROWN
STORY OF THE SEASON

MATCHDAY 21

King Power Stadium, 14.01.17
LEICESTER CITY 0 CHELSEA 3
Alonso 6, 51, Pedro 71

Marcos Alonso became the third Chelsea defender to net a Premier League brace and Pedro scored his fourth goal in as many games to move the Blues seven points clear at the top of the table.

Having beaten Leicester City twice already this season, we made a perfect start at the King Power Stadium when Eden Hazard, playing as the striker in our 3-4-2-1 system, teed up Alonso to curl a tidy right-footed shot past Kasper Schmeichel after only six minutes.

The Foxes responded well and it required some resolute defending to keep them out for the remainder of the half, but another early goal after the interval proved crucial. Alonso was the scorer once again, this time on his favoured left foot and with the aid of a couple of deflections.

With 20 minutes remaining, Pedro set up Willian with a cheeky backheel and though the Brazilian's shot was kept out, the Blues No11 was on hand to head into an empty net from the rebound.

MATCHDAY 22

Stamford Bridge, 22.01.17
CHELSEA 2 HULL CITY 0
Diego Costa 45+7, Cahill 81

Late goals in either half helped the Blues move eight points clear at the top of the Premier League table on a weekend when the majority of the chasing pack dropped points.

Diego Costa returned to the starting line-up after missing the win at Leicester and within 10 seconds of kick-off he had fizzed a shot just wide of the target, but much of the first-half was a stop-start affair and it took until stoppage time for the deadlock to be broken.

The Blues' No19 was the scorer, taking his tally for the season to 15 with a crisp, low finish after Victor Moses had surged down the right and delivered a pin-point pass across the penalty area.

Hull's second-half performance ensured the victory was far from a foregone conclusion, but the visitors were largely restricted to shots from distance, which Thibaut Courtois confidently dealt with.

The clincher finally came in the final 10 minutes as Cesc Fàbregas's free-kick was headed home by Gary Cahill.

David Luiz slides on his knees in celebration after netting a free-kick against Liverpool

RECLAIMING THE CROWN
STORY OF THE SEASON

MATCHDAY 23

Anfield, 31.01.17

LIVERPOOL 1 CHELSEA 1

Wijnaldum 57 · David Luiz 25

David Luiz marked his 100th Premier League appearance with his first goal since returning to the Blues and, though a late penalty miss by Diego Costa meant we had to settle for a draw, our nearest challengers also dropped points on Tuesday night.

With a 10-point advantage over the Reds going into the game, Chelsea were content to soak up pressure and hit the home side on the counter-attack. The tactic worked a treat midway through the first half when Eden Hazard drew a foul from Adam Lallana and David Luiz stepped up to strike a stunning quick free-kick in off the post.

Although the equaliser came early in the second period from the head of Georginio Wijnaldum, the Blues had a chance to win it late on when Diego Costa surged forward and was tripped by Joel Matip in the box. The Chelsea No19 stepped up to take the penalty himself, but a fine save by Simon Mignolet, low to his right, ensured it finished honours even.

MATCHDAY 24

Stamford Bridge, 04.02.17

CHELSEA 3 ARSENAL 1

Alonso 13, Hazard 53, Fàbregas 85 · Giroud 90+1

Chelsea won our 11th home game on the bounce to send Arsenal away from west London pointless for the fifth consecutive season.

The Blues went ahead in the first half through Marcos Alonso, who showed unbelievable desire to beat Hector Bellerin to the loose ball and head home from close range after Diego Costa's header had come back off the crossbar.

Thibaut Courtois played his part with a fine save to deny Gabriel, but the moment of the match came after the half-time break courtesy of the twinkle-toed Eden Hazard. The Belgian danced his way through the Arsenal defence, showing remarkable balance throughout before sending his shot past Petr Cech – and earning Hazard our Goal of the Season award.

Cesc Fàbregas came off the bench to lob the ball over the Czech keeper, whose misplaced pass gifted him possession, for our third of the afternoon. Although Olivier Giroud headed a stoppage-time goal for the Gunners, it was little more than a consolation for Arsene Wenger's side.

Marcos Alonso heads home the opener against Arsenal

KERRY BLUES
CHELSEA FOOTBALL CLUB
YOKOHAMA
Emirates

FABREGAS
4
BETEASY
joma
YOKOHAMA

Cesc Fàbregas keeps his balance to score against Swansea

RECLAIMING THE CROWN
STORY OF THE SEASON

MATCHDAY 25

Turf Moor, 12.02.17

BURNLEY 1 CHELSEA 1

Brady 24 · Pedro 7

Although Pedro gave us the perfect start at Turf Moor, the Blues were pegged back by a spectacular Robbie Brady free-kick as we were held to a draw by the side with the third-best home record in the Premier League.

A strong start by Antonio Conte's men saw Eden Hazard almost open the scoring after being sent through on goal – but we only had to wait another minute to break the deadlock.

Victor Moses was heavily involved, evading one challenge down the right-hand side before squaring for Pedro to direct a precise shot beyond the reach of Tom Heaton.

However, the home side were back on level terms midway through the half when Brady curled a set-piece into the top corner, the first goal we had conceded from a direct free-kick in the Premier League since March 2013. Despite enjoying more than two-thirds of possession, we were unable to breach the Clarets' well-drilled defence, but the result still secured an eight-point advantage at the top of the table.

MATCHDAY 26

Stamford Bridge, 25.02.17

CHELSEA 3 SWANSEA CITY 1

Fàbregas 19, Pedro 72, Diego Costa 84 · Llorente 45+2

Cesc Fàbregas marked his 300th Premier League game with a goal which, with the addition of late strikes from Pedro and Diego Costa, helped the Blues to a 10th top-flight home win on the bounce.

Chelsea's No4 took less than 20 minutes to mark the milestone appearance in style as he applied the finishing touch to a brilliant team move to give us a lead our early dominance merited. Our front three were all involved in the build-up, which culminated in Pedro teeing up Fàbregas to prod the ball into the far corner.

Swansea levelled against the run of play on the stroke of half-time when Fernando Llorente headed home a free-kick, but we started strongly after the break and our pressure eventually told when Pedro netted from 25 yards.

The third goal arrived soon after when Eden Hazard brilliantly teed up Diego Costa for his customary strike against the Swans, making it eight in five appearances against the side from South Wales.

Diego Costa scores from close range at the London Stadium

MATCHDAY 27

London Stadium, 06.03.17

WEST HAM UNITED 1 CHELSEA 2

Lanzini 90+2 · Hazard 25, Diego Costa 50

Goals either side of half-time from Eden Hazard and Diego Costa secured our 21st Premier League victory of the season to maintain our advantage at the top of the table.

The Blues went in front midway through the opening half with a stunning effort on the counter-attack. There looked to be little threat to the Hammers' back-line when N'Golo Kanté won possession deep in his own territory, but within three passes – the last of which was played by Pedro – Hazard was in on goal and slotting the ball past Darren Randolph for a brilliant opener.

We doubled our advantage shortly after the interval. The home side failed to deal with an inswinging corner from Cesc Fàbregas and Diego Costa was left completely unmarked at the back post to turn the ball in with his thigh from just a couple of yards out.

The only blot on our copybook came deep into stoppage time when Manuel Lanzini slotted home, but it proved to be little more than a consolation goal.

MATCHDAY 28

Bet365 Stadium, 18.03.17

STOKE CITY 1 CHELSEA 2

Walters pen 38 · Willian 13, Cahill 87

A poacher's finish by centre-back Gary Cahill gave the Blues a deserved win over Stoke City to keep us 10 points clear of the chasing pack.

After our thrilling 4-2 victory in the corresponding fixture at the Bridge to close out 2016, this was another impressive performance against the Potters – and once again it featured a goal from Willian. After netting twice in that game, the Brazilian displayed his prowess from set-pieces with a clever effort to catch out goalkeeper Lee Grant at his near post.

However, the visitors were gifted a leveller shortly before the break when Cahill was harshly adjudged to have fouled Jon Walters in the box. The striker, who once scored two own goals and missed a penalty in the same game against the Blues, made no mistake from 12 yards on this occasion.

Our efforts, including a Marcos Alonso free-kick which cannoned off the bar, looked to be in vain until Cahill showed great composure inside the box to sweep home from close range.

STOKE CITY
1863
THE POTTERS
CHELSEA
FOOTBALL CLUB
The Q-railing Stand
GRANT
WWW.Q-RAILING.COM

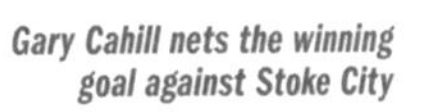

Gary Cahill nets the winning goal against Stoke City

ETIHAD
DROGBA

Eden Hazard scores his second in our win over Manchester City

RECLAIMING THE CROWN
STORY OF THE SEASON

MATCHDAY 29

Stamford Bridge, 01.04.17
CHELSEA 1 CRYSTAL PALACE 2
Fàbregas 5 · Zaha 9, Benteke 11

Chelsea suffered our first defeat at Stamford Bridge since September despite taking an early lead in this London derby against Crystal Palace.

The Blues got off to a perfect start in the fifth minute of the contest when Cesc Fàbregas prodded home from close range via the left-hand post, a goal which came after Eden Hazard had jinked and feinted his way to the byline before teeing up the Spaniard.

However, the lead proved to be shortlived as the visitors drew level just four minutes later after Wilfried Zaha found a yard of space to drive a low shot into the far corner of the net. The Ivorian winger was involved once again as Palace scored a quick-fire second, playing in Christian Benteke to dink the ball over Thibaut Courtois.

Chelsea came close to an equaliser on numerous occasions, but the Eagles' defence remained resolute and Wayne Hennessey was in inspired form to repel any shots which made their way through.

MATCHDAY 30

Stamford Bridge, 05.04.17
CHELSEA 2 MANCHESTER CITY 1
Hazard 10, 35 · Aguero 26

Two goals from Eden Hazard capped an excellent team performance as the Blues became the first club to do the league double over a side managed by Pep Guardiola.

Chelsea's Belgian ace got us off to a perfect start when he opened the scoring after only 10 minutes. Spanish duo Pedro and Cesar Azpilicueta combined down the right-hand side for the latter to send a low cross into the path of Hazard, who confidently fired home.

Cesc Fàbregas almost doubled our lead when his deflected shot bounced off the crossbar, but City were level soon after through Sergio Aguero following a misplaced clearance by Thibaut Courtois.

The response from Antonio Conte's side was decisive, however. The Blues were awarded a penalty when Pedro was brought down by Fernandinho and though Hazard saw his spot-kick saved by Willy Caballero, he turned in the rebound to put us in front. A solid second-half display ensured we ground out a win which gave us our 10th Premier League double over City.

YOKOHAMA
TYRES
19

Marcos Alonso turns away in delight after scoring a free-kick at the Vitality Stadium

MATCHDAY 31

Vitality Stadium, 08.04.17

BOURNEMOUTH 1 CHELSEA 3

King 42 · A Smith own goal 17, Hazard 20, Alonso 68

Two goals in three first-half minutes proved to be the difference between the sides in an entertaining encounter on the South Coast.

After a relatively slow start, the Blues burst into life just past the quarter-hour mark and took the lead courtesy of Diego Costa's deflected effort. Although there was a touch of fortune about it, with a skewed shot going in off the head of the sliding Adam Smith, who was credited with the goal, the turn by the Chelsea No19 was world class.

A few minutes later, N'Golo Kanté brilliantly picked out the run of Eden Hazard, who surged forward and left Artur Boruc on his backside with a superb touch before slotting home with his left foot.

Bournemouth halved the deficit on the stroke of half-time when Joshua King's ferocious shot flew into the top corner off the knee of David Luiz. However, the Blues restored our two-goal cushion in the 68th minute when Marcos Alonso brilliantly curled home a free-kick.

MATCHDAY 32

Old Trafford, 16.04.17

MANCHESTER UNITED 2 CHELSEA 0

Rashford 7, Herrera 49

Early goals in either half condemned Chelsea to our first defeat against Manchester United since October 2012.

The Blues were unfortunate to fall behind early on as a clear handball by Ander Herrera went unpunished before the Spaniard sent Marcus Rashford through on goal to finish past Asmir Begovic, who was playing his first Premier League match of the season due to an injury to Thibaut Courtois.

The closest we came to testing David de Gea in the first half was a thumping long-range effort by Diego Costa which was just wide of the post, but our task became even greater just four minutes after the break when Herrera's strike from the edge of the box was deflected past the unfortunate Begovic.

Despite a change in formation and the introduction of fresh faces, there was to be no rousing comeback by Antonio Conte's side on a frustrating Easter Sunday afternoon in Manchester as we slipped to our first defeat against the Red Devils in 13 matches.

19
Virgin

Diego Costa heads in our third goal against Southampton

RECLAIMING THE CROWN
STORY OF THE SEASON

MATCHDAY 33

Stamford Bridge, 25.04.17

CHELSEA 4 SOUTHAMPTON 2

Hazard 5, Cahill 45+1, Diego Costa 54, 89 · Romeu 24, Bertrand 90+4

Gary Cahill, Diego Costa and Eden Hazard provided all four goals between them to see off the Saints at Stamford Bridge.

It was Hazard who opened the scoring just five minutes in with a placed finish into the bottom corner from the edge of the box after receiving Diego Costa's pull-back.

Oriol Romeu equalised from a corner as the visitors came to life midway through the opening period, but right on the stroke of half-time Cahill headed us back in front.

Diego Costa grabbed his 50th Premier League goal for the Blues early in the second half after nodding in Cesc Fàbregas' pinpoint cross. Our No19 gave us a three-goal margin with the best of the game, exchanging passes with Hazard and Pedro before weaving through defenders into the penalty box and finishing smartly at Fraser Forster's near post.

Ex-Chelsea player Ryan Bertrand netted the third headed goal of the game in stoppage time, earning a sporting round of applause from the home fans.

MATCHDAY 34

Goodison Park, 30.04.17

EVERTON 0 CHELSEA 3

Pedro 66, Cahill 79, Willian 86

Second-half goals from Pedro, Gary Cahill and Willian earned Chelsea a valuable three points at Goodison Park as we remained firmly in charge of the title race.

The Blues had to be patient and saw out a bright opening from the hosts, with Dominic Calvert-Lewin going the closest to breaking the deadlock when he struck the post.

The Blues took control of proceedings after the interval, with the opener coming from Pedro. After receiving the ball 25 yards out with his back to goal, the Spaniard turned Phil Jagielka before curling a sublime left-footed effort into the top corner.

Our second had a touch of good fortune about it, when Everton keeper Maarten Stekelenburg could only parry Hazard's free-kick onto Gary Cahill inside the six-yard box and the rebound went in to give the defender his second goal in as many games. Willian completed the scoring in the dying stages, slotting the ball into the back of the net after good work by Cesc Fàbregas.

Everton
1878
NIL SATIS NISI OPTIMUM
CHELSEA
FOOTBALL CLUB
dafabet
DAVIES
26
dafabet

Pedro opens the scoring against Everton

GUZAN
12
FC.COM
Supporters Club

Nemanja Matic scores our third goal against Middlesbrough

RECLAIMING THE CROWN

STORY OF THE SEASON

MATCHDAY 35

Stamford Bridge, 08.05.17

CHELSEA 3 MIDDLESBROUGH 0

Diego Costa 23, Alonso 34, Matic 65

There only looked one likely winner of this match right from the start, with Marcos Alonso rattling the woodwork inside the first 90 seconds of a dominant display against Middlesbrough.

It was therefore something of a surprise it took as long as 23 minutes for Chelsea to open the scoring, Diego Costa providing the breakthrough by casually rolling the ball between Brad Guzan's legs from close range.

Ten minutes later the lead was doubled when Cesar Azpilicueta played the ball behind the Boro defence for Alonso to finish off.

The Blues piled on more pressure in the second half, Pedro hitting the crossbar within a minute of the restart, but it was Nemanja Matic who put the result beyond doubt, calmly completing a slick passing move involving Eden Hazard, David Luiz and Fàbregas.

The victory, our 300th at home in the Premier League, confirmed Middlesbrough's relegation from the top flight.

MATCHDAY 36

The Hawthorns, 12.05.17

WEST BROMWICH ALBION 0 CHELSEA 1

Batshuayi 82

The Blues sealed our second Premier League in three seasons thanks to a hard-fought victory over West Brom, as Michy Batshuayi's late goal at the Hawthorns clinched the title for us with two games to spare.

Antonio Conte's side knew three points in the Black Country would secure our fifth Premier League crown, but it looked like our chase would go into the final week of the campaign as we were met by a resilient Throstles rearguard.

West Brom keeper Ben Foster was regularly called into action, but it appeared as if the home side would stand firm and keep the Blues waiting to celebrate glory.

However, there was no doubting the hero of the evening. Batshuayi was pitched into action late on and he was perfectly placed to turn home Cesar Azpilicueta's early cross from six yards out.

Fans, players and staff celebrated long into the night at the Hawthorns. It had truly been a collective effort to restore Chelsea to the top of the English football tree.

WEST BROMWICH
ALBION
CHELSEA
FOOTBALL CLUB
YOKOHAMA
TYRES

Michy Batshuayi clinches the Premier League title for the Blues with this goal against West Brom

John Terry jumps for joy after scoring his 67th Chelsea goal in the victory against Watford

RECLAIMING THE CROWN
STORY OF THE SEASON

MATCHDAY 37

Stamford Bridge, 15.05.17

CHELSEA 4 WATFORD 3

Terry 22, Azpilicueta 36, Batshuayi 49, Fàbregas 88 · Capoue 24, Janmaat 51, Okaka 74

Chelsea's first game at Stamford Bridge since clinching the Premier League title was a seven-goal thriller settled by substitute Cesc Fàbregas' late winner.

John Terry got the ball rolling with a typically instinctive finish, scoring for the 17th season in a row in the English top flight and bringing up our century for the campaign in all competitions.

Although Etienne Capoue brought Watford level soon after, our lead was restored before the break by Cesar Azpilicueta. He became our 14th different scorer of the season in the league with a drilled finish from the edge of the box after a corner was cleared to him.

Fresh from his title-clinching goal, Michy Batshuayi netted just after half-time with the simplest of finishes after brilliantly being teed up by Nathan Ake, but our two-goal lead was wiped out by Daryl Janmaat and Stefano Okaka.

However, a 16th Premier League home win of the season was secured by Fàbregas, whose scuffed finish on the edge of the box just evaded the dive of Heurelho Gomes.

The players show their appreciation to Antonio Conte at the end of the match

EU5
EU6
FOOTBALL CLUB
THAILAND BLUES
CHELSEA FC OFFICIAL SUPPORTERS CLUB
AUSTIN BLUES
SOUTHEAST BLUES
FROM LONDON TO THE SOUTHEAST, USA
QUEENSLAND
EM6
HOME OF THE CHAMPIONS
ANTONIO CONTE
FOR
PRIME MINISTER

RECLAIMING THE CROWN
STORY OF THE SEASON

MATCHDAY 38

Stamford Bridge, 21.05.17

CHELSEA 5 SUNDERLAND 1

Willian 8, Hazard 61, Pedro 77, Batshuayi 90, 90+2 · Manquillo 3

The chants of "Antoniooo!" had already been swirling around Stamford Bridge for months when, on the final day of a triumphant 2016/17 season, the manager stepped into the technical area and raised his arms in recognition as all four stands sang his name in unison. This scene had played out on several previous occasions, but this time Antonio Conte was able to enjoy it that bit more. After all, he was just minutes away from collecting the Premier League trophy, alongside his players, at the end of his first year in English football.

By that point, of course, the title celebrations were already well underway. They had begun in the West Midlands nine days earlier when Michy Batshuayi had emerged from the bench to score the only goal of a tense game away at West Bromwich Albion with just eight minutes to go, and make himself a Blues hero. At the final whistle, the party started in the away end of The Hawthorns, in the pubs of west London

The title celebrations at West Brom

VICTOR MOSES

"It's the happiest day of my life, I'm absolutely buzzing. The most important thing was winning the 30 games, we took that very seriously so we're really happy."

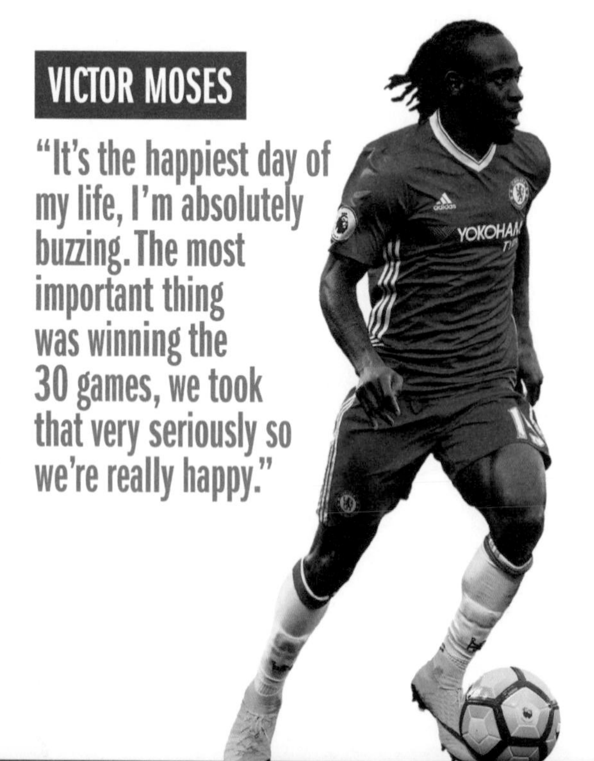

and in Chelsea living rooms all over the world. That 1-0 win – one of six straight victories to end the league season – confirmed Chelsea as champions of England for the sixth time.

The players danced in front of the travelling Blues supporters, joined them for a singsong and took it in turns to be thrown into the air by their delirious team-mates. The scenes that followed in the dressing room have been shared across social media, captured by the champagne-soaked TV camera lenses and mobile phones, shaking as they bounced up and down in the players' hands.

"The togetherness this group has shown from day one is special," John Terry reflected, proudly. "Even when we lost games early on – to Liverpool at home and Arsenal away – we showed great togetherness to regroup and come back strong. That winning streak we went on was incredible. I think it was fundamental in our season."

It was the first time since our first Premier League success in 2005 that we had sealed the title away from home but the final two games of the season were at Stamford Bridge, and this year's title salute became a three-stage celebration.

Friday night's euphoria had carried over to Monday in the shape of an impromptu lap of honour after the dramatic win over Watford. Symbolically, an inflatable crown, thrown from the stands, had become the prop of choice for Conte and his players as they bounced and cheered their way around the pitch while fireworks lit up a balmy west London night sky.

Then Sunday arrived, and with it Sunderland, but nobody was thinking about the opposition, in truth. In fact, this was a day that many fans found it hard to get their heads around: John Terry's last Chelsea appearance, and it would end in him becoming the first person to lift the Premier League trophy for a fifth time as captain.

He led the team out for his 717th and final Chelsea game accompanied by his two children, George and Summer, as the familiar ring of Harry J. Allstars' The Liquidator filled the stadium. He looked up to see a display of thanks covering the Shed End and a giant flag in his honour passing across the Matthew Harding Stand. After 22 years at the club he had joined as a 14-year-old, it was time for the most successful player in Chelsea's history to sign off.

In his last performance he was pure JT: pointing, leading, pushing forward with the ball at his feet and fighting for every loose ball. Then, when the 26th minute arrived, it was time for the man who has worn the No26 shirt for

Champions
2016/17
EVER SEEN
CHELSEA
WIN THE LEAGUE
SAFFRON
BLUES
CHELSEA
FOOTBALL CLUB
CHELSEA
FOOTBALL
CLUB
THE SHED END

CHELSEA FOOTBALL CLUB
SUNDERLAND A.F.C.
Premier League
adidas
OHAMA
TYRES

RECLAIMING THE CROWN

every one of his first-team appearances to make his exit. The crowd rose to their feet, team-mates and opponents alike rushed to hug and congratulate him, and then the Chelsea players formed a guard of honour for him as he left the Stamford Bridge pitch one last time in our colours.

There was still the lion's share of a football match to be played, however, and the Bridge was charged with so many positive emotions that humid spring afternoon. The departure of JT had brought tears to eyes and lumps to throats, but the title-party atmosphere was still alive in the stands. It brought the best out of the players on the pitch, too.

Even now, on the final day of the campaign, when they had already wrapped things up with two matches to spare, Conte's men refused to take their foot off the gas. They were aware that they needed to emerge victorious from both of those remaining fixtures to become the first team to win 30 games in a Premier League season. After going a goal down just three minutes in, to a Sunderland side with a point to

THIBAUT COURTOIS

"It's nice for the players that all the work we've done this season counts for something and means we get to have this amazing feeling again. I live for these moments of joy and excitement."

John Terry is given a guard of honour as he leaves the pitch

prove, the Blues showed their determination to secure that landmark 30th win and see their captain off in fitting fashion.

Willian levelled on eight minutes and, for a while after Terry's substitution, the game seemed to continue in the background somewhat as the supporters gathered themselves and sang their departing hero's name. Then, after the break, Chelsea came alive. A week before he was named the supporters' Player of the Year, Eden Hazard nabbed his 17th goal of the season to put us 2-1 ahead on the hour, before Pedro came off the bench to pounce on a defensive mix-up and register his 13th goal of 2016/17.

It was that kind of season – even with the league won, we could not take our eyes off the pitch for a moment, and the hero of the final month of the season, Batshuayi, scored the last two goals of the 85 we managed over the course of the league season in the 90th and 92nd minutes of the final game. A 5-1 victory, and then they gave us the trophy, lifted by Terry and Cahill in the middle

CESC FABREGAS

"I've been very lucky to win things, probably the biggest things in football, but winning the Premier League gives you a special feeling. This is the best league in the world."

Eden Hazard puts us ahead against Sunderland

Pedro nets our third goal of the game

DAVID LUIZ

"When I decided to come back here it was because of this – I dreamed of one day winning the Premier League so I'm very happy because my dream came true."

Michy Batshuayi celebrates scoring our fourth goal

of the pitch. The outgoing captain summed up his emotions quite perfectly when he was handed the microphone after the game.

"The best supporters in the world without a doubt," Terry said, stood amidst the ribbons and streamers that lay strewn across the pitch after the trophy presentation. "Thank you will never ever be enough. I am going to come back here one day, supporting this team. I love you all."

The chants of his name rose up between every sentence he uttered, as they had done every few minutes during the game, and it was fitting that he was able to bow out on a successful note, that his last act as a Chelsea player was to lift the Premier League trophy and then bounce around with his team-mates to Madness' One Step Beyond. Surely that was the best farewell gift he could have hoped for: Chelsea, champions of England 2016/17.

JOHN TERRY

"What an unbelievable feeling and, believe me, it just gets better and better. I'm so proud of this team and all the players and management for all the hard work, effort and sacrifices everyone has made this season."

YOKOHAMA
TYRES
Premier League

CHELSEA
FOOTBALL CLUB
SUNDERLAND A.F.C.

YOKOHAMA TYRES
Premier League
CC
Carabao

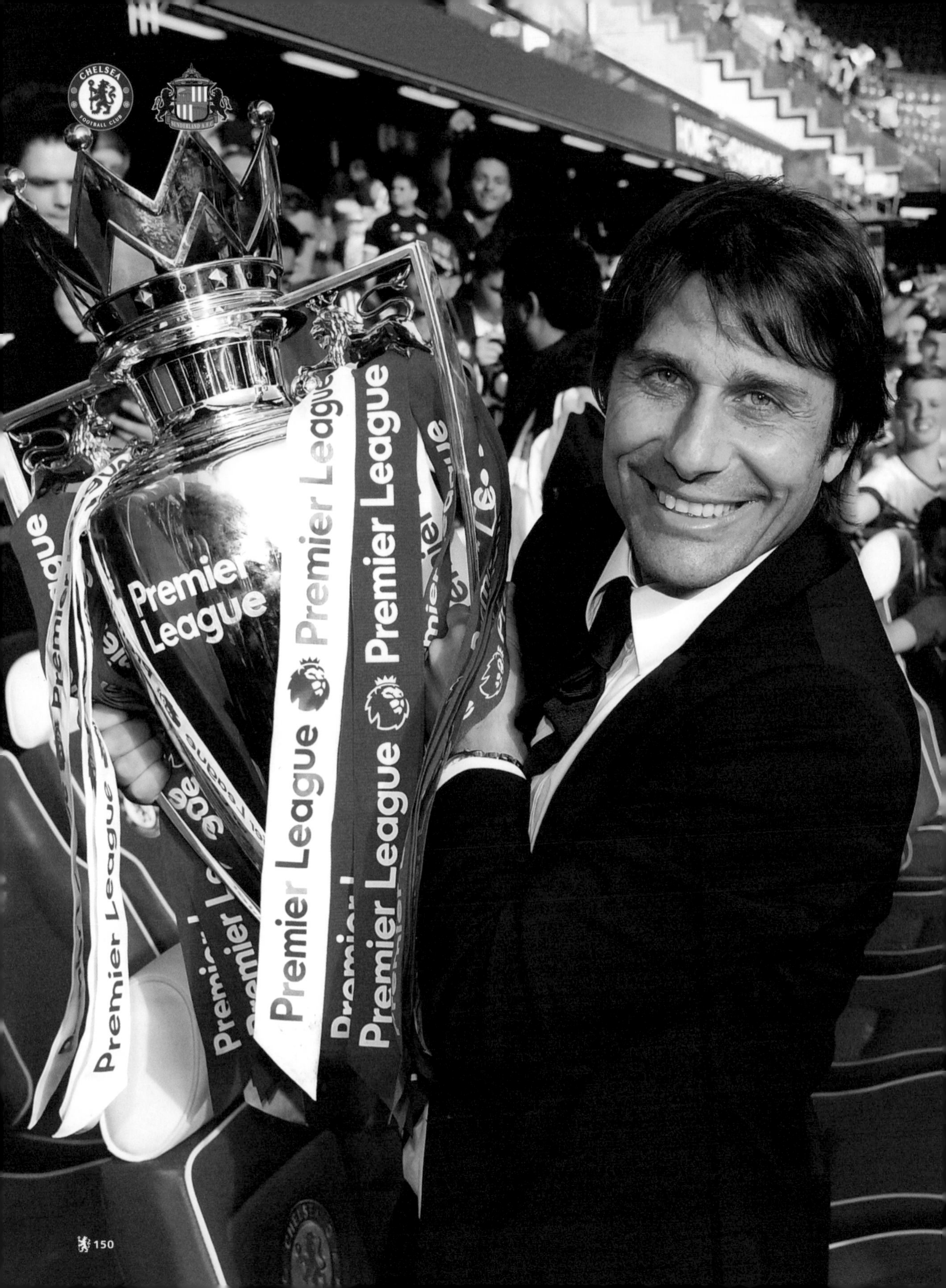
Premier League
Premier League
Premier League

ANTONIO CONTE

"We have worked so hard this season to be at the top of the league and now we can enjoy it. This group has given me so much. We have only been working together for nine months and yet we are champions. There is room to improve and to grow and we are looking forward to doing that because we all share the same ambitions. It is great to have these moments, to see what it means to our supporters and to enjoy our success."

League
League
Premier
CHELSEA
FOOTBALL CLUB
Premier League

7

N'GOLO KANTE

Nobody has received as much praise for their part in Chelsea's 2016/17 title triumph as N'Golo Kanté. A succession of awards rained on the Frenchman during the latter stages of the season, including being named the PFA, FWA and Premier League's Player of the Year.

His constant energy and ability to regain possession for the team, both with his persistent tackling and frequent interceptions, made him an invaluable asset for Antonio Conte as he rebuilt the Blues in his own footballing philosophy.

Having Kanté in your side has often been compared to having 12 players on the pitch, and that capability to cover so much ground has been vital in a system that requires such constant adjusting of position to fill gaps and cover your team-mates when defending.

His all-action style also complemented his midfield partners perfectly, whether that was giving Cesc Fàbregas the cover he needed to push forward or combining his mobility with Nemanja Matic's strength to hunt the ball as a pair.

It is fair to say every single player in the team benefited from Kanté's presence on the pitch. He gave them the confidence to take chances on the ball or rush forward to join the attack, safe in the knowledge that the man covering their back was the best in the business.

Although it was his defensive efforts which won him the majority of his praise, Kanté wasn't shy of showing his own attacking talent. When the situation presented itself, the French international displayed an impressive range of passing to help launch attacks. He also undertook the occasional foray forward, most notably to score two excellent goals against Manchester United at Stamford Bridge, slaloming through their defence in the Premier League in October for the first and beating David de Gea from outside the box in our FA Cup quarter-final in March for the second.

Carabao

YOKOHAMA
TYRES

YOKOHAMA TYRES
William HILL
sky SPORTS
FWA

“I don’t pretend to be like Ramires or Makelele. I just go my way in football and try to do my best. I just do it my way, try to improve and try to do my best.”

CONTE SAYS...

"I think he's a complete midfielder, not only a defensive midfielder. He's a player that always arrives in the box and he has fantastic stamina, good technique and also good positioning and good personality."

STATS...

N'Golo Kanté is the only person to have played in the Premier League for the champions in successive seasons, with different clubs. Having played a key role in Leicester City's shock title win in 2015/16, he repeated the trick by helping us to glory in the following campaign. Only one other player has claimed back-to-back titles with different clubs and they also did it with Chelsea and Leicester, in 2014/15 and 2015/16, but Mark Schwarzer didn't appear for either side in the Premier League in their winning seasons.

N'GOLO KANTE	
Position: Midfielder	
Date of birth: 29.03.91	
Place of birth: Paris, France	
2016/17 PREMIER LEAGUE	
Appearances	35
Minutes	3341
Goals	1
Assists	3

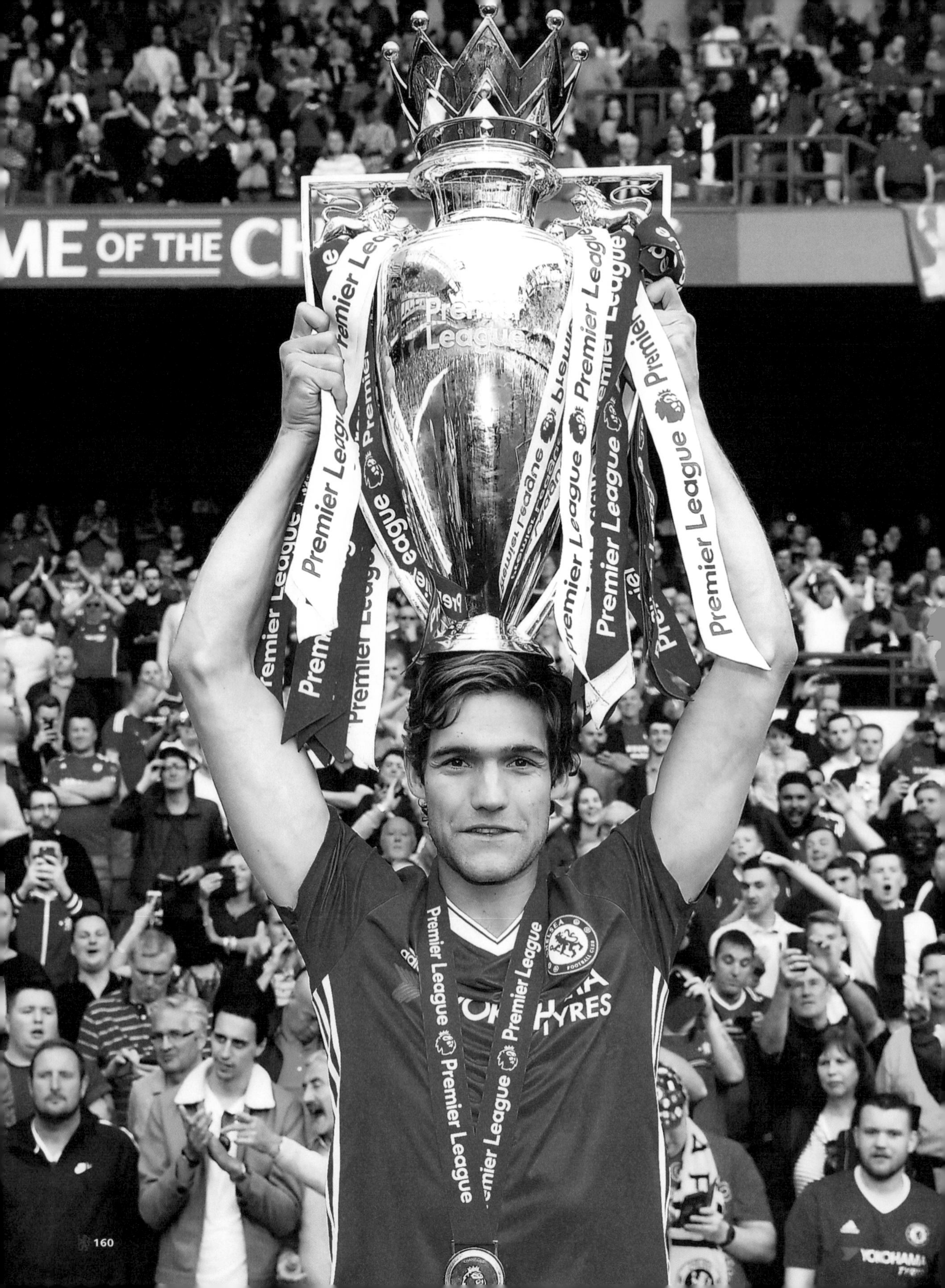
ME OF THE CH
Premier League

3

MARCOS ALONSO

If ever a player's emergence coincided with an upturn in Chelsea's fortunes quite like Marcus Alonso's, it's hard to say. He entered the fray early in the second half against Arsenal in September with the Blues already 3-0 down as Antonio Conte switched to his preferred 3-4-2-1 formation for the first time.

Though that match ended in defeat, it was the wing-back system which transformed the Blues' season and Alonso's marauding displays down the left were the source of much joy from then on.

Conte fielded the new formation from the start for the first time in our 2-0 victory at Hull, Alonso's full debut following his summer switch from Fiorentina.

That was the beginning of a club-record sequence of 13 consecutive league wins, with Alonso featuring in all those games as the Blues swept to the top of the table. As the New Year began with a 2-0 defeat at Tottenham, it was the time for cool heads and Alonso proved to be the man for the occasion when we travelled to reigning champions Leicester. The press may have had their knives sharpened, but Alonso was superb in a 3-0 win that highlighted his ever-growing attacking threat.

The Spaniard netted twice and was unlucky not to score a hat-trick as he collected the Man of the Match award and the Blues established a seven-point margin at the summit. That all six of his goals came in the Premier League is a rubber stamp on the fact Alonso's contribution to Chelsea's triumphant 2016/17 campaign cannot be underestimated.

However, it would be misguided to think the Spaniard is solely focused on going forward. With incredible stamina, he consistently showed the ability to fulfil his defensive duties. He acknowledged that his previous Premier League experience with Bolton Wanderers and Sunderland helped his adaptation.

Plus, with football pedigree running through his veins – his father and grandfather were Spanish internationals – he displayed intelligence, bringing great balance to the side.

YOKOHAMA
TYRES
YOKOHAMA
TYRES

YOKOHAMA
TYRES
Premier League

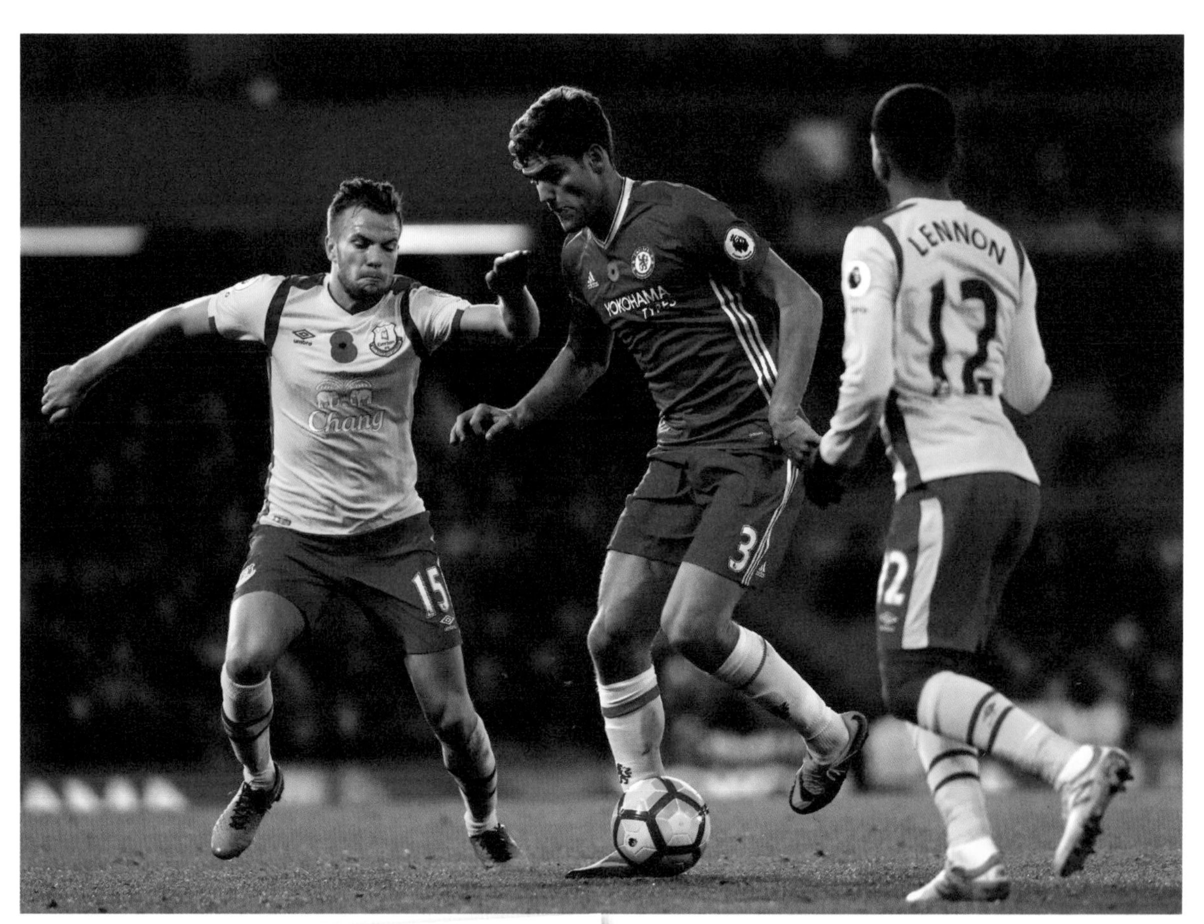
LENNON
12
YOKOHAMA
15
3
Chang

HELSEA FOOTBALL CLUB
YOKOHAMA TYRES
adidas

"It's my first big trophy, very special. Also, to get 30 wins is a new record as well. We've been working hard all year, the manager has done a great job and he's had every player focused on our objective, which was the title. I'm very happy."

YOKOHAMA TYRES
He makes me down to lie, In pastures green; He
CECH
33

CONTE SAYS...

"His contribution, it's great. Marcos, I think, is one of the players who has grown this season. He worked a lot to improve and his attitude and work-rate is great. Don't forget that, when Alonso arrived at Chelsea, he wasn't playing. Then he started to play and deserved to start every game."

STATS...

As well as contributing an impressive six league goals in 2016/17, Alonso also provided three assists in the Premier League. His willingness to get forward is highlighted by the fact he had the fifth-highest number of shots on goal in the Chelsea squad (36), with 44 per cent of his efforts on target.

MARCOS ALONSO	
Position: Defender	
Date of birth: 28.12.90	
Place of birth: Madrid, Spain	
2016/17 PREMIER LEAGUE	
Appearances	30+1
Minutes	2860
Goals	6
Assists	3

adidas
Premier League

19

DIEGO COSTA

For an indication of just how effective Diego Costa was during the 2016/17 season, one statistic does the job: no player's goals secured more Premier League points for his team than the Blues' No19.

While the race for the Golden Boot went down to a straight fight between winner Harry Kane and Romelu Lukaku, both players made a habit of scoring their goals in clusters – the Belgian, for example, had five multiple-goal games, compared to just two for Diego Costa, while Kane netted four hat-tricks.

The Spain international was decisive from the first fixture, when he scored late on against West Ham to turn one point into three, and repeated the trick a few days later with the winner at Watford. It was in November and December that Diego Costa's scoring made the biggest difference, though, as he netted the only goal in 1-0 wins over Middlesbrough, West Bromwich Albion and Crystal Palace. Not a month of the league season went by without him hitting the net, a record only previously achieved by 15 players, and the number of times he netted in the latter stages of either half highlights the strength of both his determination and his fitness. But there was so much more to his game than the 20-goal haul.

The moments when a game is in the balance are those when Diego Costa truly comes to the fore. Watch the intensity of his pressing as he inspires his fellow attackers to do likewise. Observe how he pursues a loose ball, or a dawdling defender, in his ceaseless efforts to unsettle opponents. It could be said many of his attributes tie in perfectly with those that Antonio Conte has instilled in the team at large.

What's more, he became the seventh player to score 50 Premier League goals for Chelsea when he netted in the 4-2 win over Southampton – and he swiftly took his tally to 51 with our fourth of the evening. He joins Frank Lampard (147), Didier Drogba (104), Jimmy Floyd Hasselbaink (69), Gianfranco Zola (59), Eden Hazard (56) and Eidur Gudjohnsen (54).

Premier League
adidas
TYRES
"YOU" - "GRAZIE"
ONE OF US

Carabao
YOKOHAMA

NAUGHTON
26
DIEGO COSTA
17

“Twenty goals is a good, solid total. Any club with a striker who is going to get 20 goals regularly, they are going to be up there competing for whatever competition they are involved in. I am not one who is looking for individual glory, it is always about scoring goals to pick up points. That is why I am looking for that consistency, that regularity of scoring, one goal every game or every other game, rather than getting three or four and then having a drought.”

DIEGO COSTA
19
McAULEY

CONTE SAYS...

"You know that Diego, for me, is the best striker in the world. It's very important to have players with good personality, with good, strong characters, because you must be ready to face a different situation. He's a warrior – but I think in the team we have a lot of warriors. I work every day to bring them to be warriors. It's great to have talent. But I like a lot when you are a warrior during the game and – above all – if players with talent show they work hard."

STATS...

Diego Costa joined an elite club with his brace against Southampton, which took him past the 20-goal mark in the Premier League for the season. Only two other players have reached that milestone figure for the Blues on two separate occasions since the English top flight was rebranded in 1992: Jimmy Floyd Hasselbaink (2000/01 and 2001/02) and Didier Drogba (2006/07 and 2009/10).

DIEGO COSTA	
Position: Forward	
Date of birth: 07.10.88	
Place of birth: Lagarto, Brazil	
2016/17 PREMIER LEAGUE	
Appearances	35
Minutes	3263
Goals	20
Assists	10

Premier League
Premier League
Premier League
CHELSEA
FOOTBALL CLUB
adidas

24

GARY CAHILL

The 2016/17 season saw Gary Cahill step up as one of the longest-serving members of the Chelsea squad and show his leadership qualities throughout the campaign. From the moment Antonio Conte switched systems to a back three, the England international was an integral part of the side playing on the left of the defence.

He put his experience to good use, too, as from the very first game using the 3-4-2-1 formation, against Hull City in October, he wore the captain's armband in every remaining Premier League match until after the title was sealed at West Bromwich Albion in May.

His contribution as acting captain on the pitch, as well as a key member of the defence, was shown first when he was officially appointed vice-captain following the departure of Branislav Ivanovic in January, and again when John Terry invited his fellow defender to join him in lifting the Premier League trophy on the final day.

In addition to being a more frequent name on the scoresheet, Cahill was the man behind some crucial goals in the title race, including his strike just before half-time to give us the lead at home against Southampton in April, as we bounced back from defeat to Manchester United in our previous match.

However, nowhere was the 31-year-old's character and strength of will more evident than at the Bet365 Stadium in March. Having conceded the penalty through which Stoke City equalised in the first half, Cahill put things right by netting our late winner himself with just three minutes left on the clock.

YOKOHAMA
TYRES
Premier League

CLUCAS
11
24
SportPesa

RAMSDENS

Carabao

“We have to cherish these moments. We’ve worked so hard all season to be where we are. Consistently, I think we’ve been the best team in the league.”

adidas
adidas
YOKOHAMA
TYRES
Carabao

CHEVROLET

CONTE SAYS...

"Gary can play also as a centre-forward! He has good quality, acrobatic qualities, and he's very good, very strong during the corners and set-pieces. Gary is our vice-captain this season, and he has put on the armband every time John did not play, and for sure Gary has the prospect to be a good captain."

STATS...

Gary Cahill enjoyed comfortably his most prolific season in front of goal in 2016/17, finding the back of the net six times in the Premier League. To put that into context, his previous best in a Premier League campaign was two and he notched up a total of seven goals in that competition in his previous four-and-a-half seasons combined.

CARY CAHILL	
Position: Defender	
Date of birth: 19.12.85	
Place of birth: Sheffield	
2016/17 PREMIER LEAGUE	
Appearances	36+1
Minutes	3507
Goals	6
Assists	0

Premier League
Premier
League
adizero

22

WILLIAN

After his eye-catching form in 2015/16, which saw him winning Player of the Year honours as selected by fans and his team-mates, Willian admitted he had an altogether more difficult campaign this time.

Having lost his mother to cancer in October, the Brazilian struggled physically and emotionally, but it is to his credit that he can still look back on the season with huge personal pride after more than playing his part in bringing silverware back from Stamford Bridge.

His free-kicks the previous season had been unerringly accurate, providing his first six goals of the campaign before November, and his wonderful form had seen him rewarded with a new four-year contract. He began the new season with a goal in our win over Burnley and he also netted the opener at Hull in the game which ushered in a new tactical dawn for the Blues. The game was goalless after an hour until the Brazilian expertly curled the ball into the top right corner of the net, but Pedro was regularly preferred at his expense as we embarked on a 13-match winning tear.

If that game showed this formation could be the way forward, his next vital contribution confirmed our place as title challengers. Brought off the bench at Manchester City, he broke clear to net the winning goal, and he also served a timely reminder of his brilliance as he netted a brace in the final game of 2016 to beat Stoke City.

Entertaining, hard-working and reliable in equal measure, he is very much the kind of player you want on your side as the season reaches the business end – and never was that more evident than in the FA Cup semi-final against Spurs. He appeared to be the calmest man on the pitch when it mattered most, netting twice in the first half; one from a trademark free-kick and the other a coolly taken penalty.

It simply added an exclamation mark to Antonio Conte's mantra that the team comes before any individual.

CHELSEA FOOTBALL
AUSTIN BLUES
YOKOHAMA TYRES

YOKOHAMA TYRES
PLAN INTERNATIONAL

“When I arrived here, always in my head was the thought of winning titles. It was my dream to come and play with Chelsea.”

Sure
Sure
Sure
✓Sur

YOKOHAMA
TYRES
22

CONTE SAYS...

"We are talking about champions, not medium players, but top players. When you have in your squad this type of player that you put in the team and he does not think of himself, but the team, it's great. Willian is one example. Pedro was playing but Willian's behaviour was always the same."

STATS...

Despite not featuring as often, Willian still managed to equal his impressive tally of 11 goals in the 2015/16 season. However, he still had three more to score to equal Oscar as Chelsea's highest-scoring Brazilian in Premier League history, although he overtook Ramires during the course of the past campaign.

WILLIAN	
Position: Midfielder	
Date of birth: 09.08.88	
Place of birth: Ribeirão Pires, São Paulo, Brazil	
2016/17 PREMIER LEAGUE	
Appearances	15+19
Minutes	1645
Goals	8
Assists	4

Premier League
Premier League
Premier League
Premier League
Premier League
Premier League
adidas

21

NEMANJA MATIC

The muscle of Nemanja Matic was regularly employed in the middle of the park by Antonio Conte during his maiden season as Blues boss. While the technical abilities of the Serbian international should not be underestimated, it has been as a midfield destroyer that he has enjoyed most of his success at Stamford Bridge, and Conte quickly understood that a strong core is needed in a competition as physical as the Premier League.

Matic has developed into an on-field leader whose influence is most often seen when we are on the back foot, but whose intelligent use of the ball when we are in the ascendancy has been quietly influential.

He brought up 100 Premier League appearances during November, by which point he had already racked up five league assists to emphasise the latter point, but there is little doubt which moment stood out above all others from his 2016/17 campaign.

It came in the latter stages of our FA Cup semi-final against Tottenham Hotspur, when Eden Hazard rolled the ball into his path 30 yards from goal and Matic let fly with a blockbuster left-footed strike which rifled into the back of the net via the crossbar, just to add to the spectacle.

While the Blues No21 let out a roar of delight as he ran towards the Chelsea supporters, he generally tried to play it cool with his celebrations; on the bench, the wide-eyed Kurt Zouma could be seen saying the words, "Oh my God" over and over as he and his fellow substitutes erupted with joy. Like the rest of us, he couldn't believe what he had witnessed – but, boy, did we enjoy seeing an unsung hero like Matic enjoying his moment in the spotlight.

Chang
YOKOHAMA

Premier
League
TYRES

21
YOKOHAMA
TYRES
34
Carabao

"You have to be very concentrated and after every game I am very tired. Sometimes, even when we have won a big game I don't have power enough left to celebrate, I just come into the changing room and sit. I need a day to recover my strength."

dafabet
YOKOHAMA
TYRES
21

YOKOHAMA

CONTE SAYS...

"With Nemanja and Cesc, we are talking about two great players with different characteristics. Nemanja is more physical, good technically and has less fantasy than Cesc. Cesc is great technically, he has great fantasy but he is less physical than Nemanja."

STATS...

Although goals are not his forte, it was still a strange quirk that Matic went into the month of May having never scored for the Blues at Stamford Bridge – especially when you consider the exquisite technique displayed in belting a shot past Hugo Lloris at Wembley in the FA Cup semi-final. Finally, the Serbian put that right against Middlesbrough, almost three-and-a-half years after he returned to Stamford Bridge in the January transfer window of 2014.

NEMANJA MATIC	
Position: Midfielder	
Date of birth: 01.08.88	
Place of birth: Šabac, Serbia	
2016/17 PREMIER LEAGUE	
Appearances	30+5
Minutes	2853
Goals	1
Assists	4

Premier League
FOOTBALL CLUB

30

DAVID LUIZ

The man in the middle of the back three for much of the season, David Luiz's return from Paris has been an unqualified success.

The Brazilian didn't manage to win the Premier League during his original spell at Chelsea but achieved it in his first year back at Stamford Bridge. He has now won the league title in Portugal, France and England.

An eternal optimist, his colourful character lifts the atmosphere wherever he goes and his ease on the ball makes him a joy to watch on the pitch, but that positivity also manifests itself in a staunch will to win.

Whether he is strolling forward with the ball at his feet and opening up the game in front of him, or firing a Ruud Gullit-style long pass into the forwards, he is as close to a playmaker as a central defender can be, but it is not just for show – he is determined to influence the game. More than that, David Luiz's strength and focus have made him an essential part of our defence.

His experience and personality make him one of the leaders in this squad and he is never awed by the big occasion. His love for the club was clear when he returned to west London last summer, and the supporters love him back. After every great intervention or pass by the bustling Brazilian, the Bridge comes alive with chants of "LUUU-IIIIIZ!"

K8凯发

YOKOHAMA
TYRES
PEDRO
11
KAN
7

JOHN TERRY
26

adidas
60
60

“We have done great since the beginning of the season… because of everybody. Because of the commitment, the desire, the mentality we put on the pitch every day. That’s why we deserve it.”

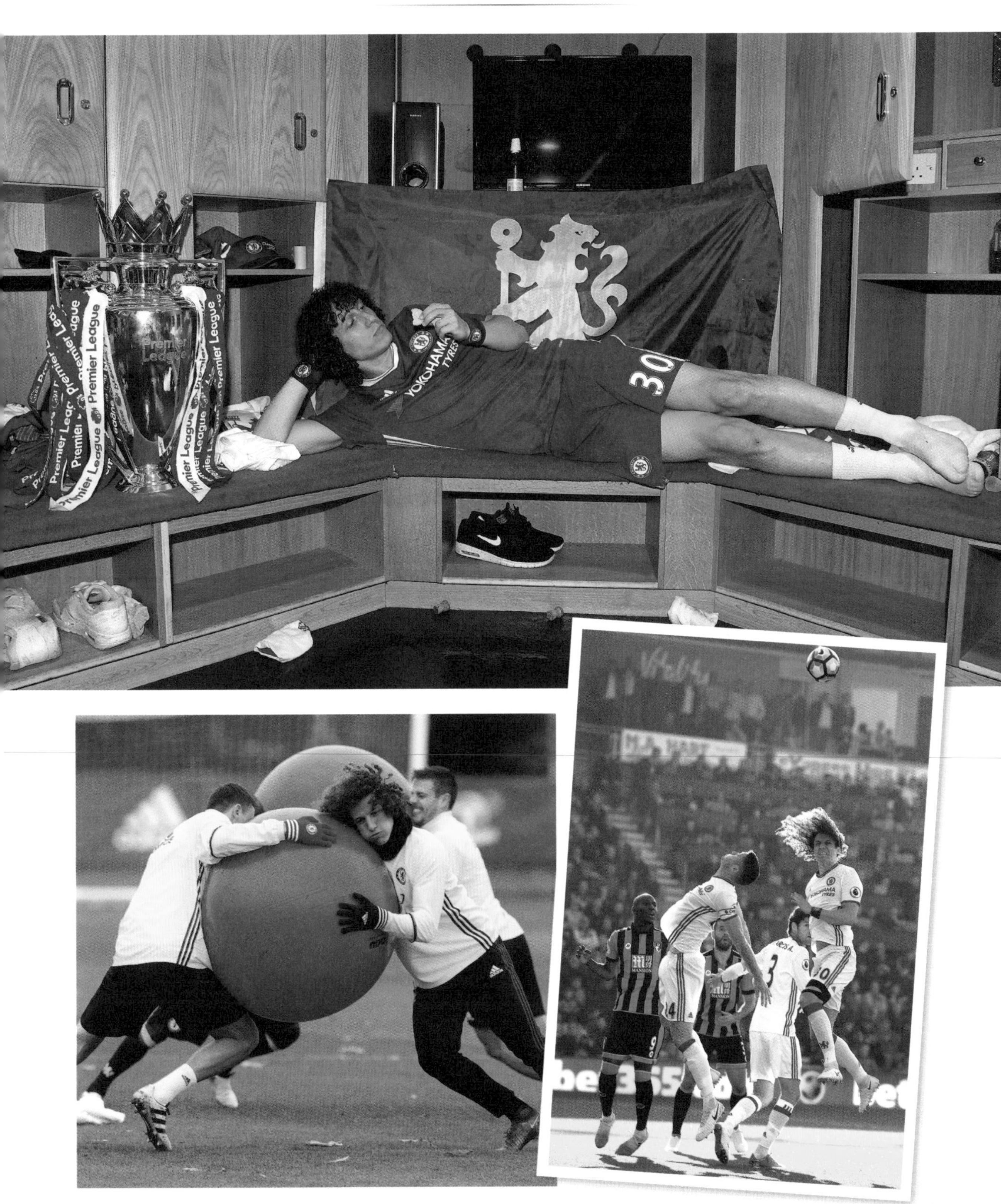
Premier League
YOKOHAMA TYRES
30

CONTE SAYS...

"I think this position is perfect for David to play as a central player in three defenders. This is the best position for him because he has good technique, he is strong, he can start our possession and he has the personality to do this."

STATS...

David Luiz's part in helping Chelsea to keep 16 clean sheets – and thereby earning Thibaut Courtois the Premier League Golden Gloves – cannot be overestimated. At the other end his only goal of the season was a stunning one, as he took a surprise free-kick to catch Liverpool completely off guard in our 1-1 draw at Anfield in January.

DAVID LUIZ	
Position: Defender	
Date of birth: 22.04.87	
Place of birth: Diadema, Brazil	
2016/17 PREMIER LEAGUE	
Appearances	33
Minutes	3141
Goals	1
Assists	2

23

MICHY BATSHUAYI

In a season when so many different players made valuable contributions to the Chelsea cause, it was fitting that a striker who had to bide his time for action was the man who clinched our fifth Premier League title against West Bromwich Albion.

By his own admission, Michy Batshuayi was an unexpected hero at The Hawthorns, and his post-match interview with Sky Sports showed just how thrilled he was to have such a telling involvement on a night that will never be forgotten.

The Belgian striker had only been on the pitch for six minutes when he slid in to convert Cesar Azpilicueta's cross and secure the three points needed for us to be champions. Despite a lack of playing time, he will always be remembered as the man who got us over the line in one of the greatest campaigns in our history.

After signing from Marseille following an impressive Euro 2016 with Belgium, when he scored with his first touch of the tournament after coming off the bench against Hungary, the 23-year-old enjoyed an encouraging start to his Chelsea career as he made a telling impact off the bench in our opening two Premier League fixtures.

In the first, at home to West Ham United, Batshuayi came on with the sides locked at 1-1 and assisted the winning goal for Diego Costa with a canny header in the 89th minute. He followed that up by scoring the first of our two goals as we came from behind to win at Watford, opening his Chelsea account from close range after Eden Hazard's strike had been parried into his path.

He was also on target against lower-league opposition in both domestic cups and started in the FA Cup semi-final win over Tottenham Hotspur, before netting in consecutive games against West Brom, Watford and Sunderland at the end of his first Premier League season.

Premier League
YOKOHAMA TYRES
23
10

OHAMA
TYRE
adidas
Carabao
Carabao

“The West Brom game was a magical moment, it’s the stuff of dreams. I am very happy to have helped the team at a big moment. I have worked very hard and I have now made a big contribution, which is a dream.”

YOKOHAMA
TYRES

CHELSEA FOOTBALL CLUB
YOKOHAMA
TYRES
adidas
Carabao

CONTE SAYS...

"I must be pleased, above all, for him. We all know the season, the difficulty he found, in this first season for him. It's not easy to play in this league, which is very strong. This league is fantastic to play and be a manager in. For him, I'm pleased because he scored goals this season. These goals were very important for him and for us. My substitutions [against West Brom] were very good – Michy repaid me a lot for this choice!"

STATS...

Batshuayi may have found Premier League minutes hard to come by, but he more than made up for it with the impact he made when he was granted playing time. His five goals in his maiden campaign in the English top flight were scored at a rate of one every 48 minutes; throw in an assist as well and it makes for positive reading for the former Marseille man.

MICHY BATSHUAYI	
Position: Forward	
Date of birth: 02.10.93	
Place of birth: Brussels, Belgium	
2016/17 PREMIER LEAGUE	
Appearances	1+19
Minutes	315
Goals	5
Assists	1

34

OLA AINA

Whatever Ola Aina goes on to achieve in football, he will long remember 2016/17, his breakthrough season in the Chelsea first-team squad.

Having made a name for himself in our Academy as a three-time FA Youth Cup winner, he started four of our six pre-season fixtures in 2016, including against Liverpool, Real Madrid and AC Milan. The versatile defender was then named on the bench for our first three Premier League matches of the season.

He made his debut from the start in our 3-2 League Cup win over Bristol Rovers in August, which was followed by a new four-year contract, and then came off the bench for his Premier League bow in October's 3-0 win at home to Leicester.

The 20-year-old also entered the fray in the Boxing Day win over Bournemouth and replaced Kenedy for the final 15 minutes of our 4-3 victory over Watford towards the end of the season.

With excellent ability on the ball and the kind of temperament that could see him go a long way under Antonio Conte's guidance, expect to see more of Aina in years to come.

OLA AINA	
Position: Defender	
Date of birth: 08.10.96	
Place of birth: Southwark	
2016/17 PREMIER LEAGUE	
Appearances	0+3
Minutes	37
Goals	0
Assists	0

37

EDUARDO

After joining Chelsea from Dinamo Zagreb in the summer of 2016, Eduardo formed an important part of the goalkeeping set-up at Cobham which allowed No1 Thibaut Courtois to flourish in our title-winning campaign.

This was recognised shortly after the season had finished as the experienced custodian signed a new one-year contract.

A model professional, Eduardo has 35 caps for Portugal and formed part of the squad which made history at the 2016 European Championship with their first major tournament triumph.

After arriving at the club, he immediately formed a strong bond with his fellow shot-stoppers, along with his other team-mates, and became a popular and respected member of the Chelsea squad.

His presence is guaranteed to have a positive influence once again next term as the Blues go in search of more silverware.

EDUARDO	
Position: Goalkeeper	
Date of birth: 19.09.82	
Place of birth: Mirandela, Portugal	
2016/17 PREMIER LEAGUE	
Appearances	0
Minutes	0
Clean sheets	0

16

KENEDY

The Brazilian wide man spent the first half of the 2016/17 season on loan at Watford, returning to the Blues in January when he made his first Chelsea appearance of the campaign as a substitute in our FA Cup victory over Brentford.

He had to wait patiently for a Premier League opportunity, which duly arrived after the title was sealed as he started in our thrilling 4-3 win over Watford.

The 21-year-old produced an energetic display in the left wing-back role which earned him warm applause from the Stamford Bridge faithful when he was taken off with 15 minutes remaining.

An affable character who shares great camaraderie with his fellow Brazilians in particular, Kenedy is a popular figure at Cobham, and with caps for his country at Under-20 and Under-22 level, he is clearly a talented prospect.

KENEDY	
Position: Wing-back	
Date of birth: 08.02.96	
Place of birth: Santa Rita do Sapucaí, Minas Gerais, Brazil	
2016/17 PREMIER LEAGUE	
Appearances	1
Minutes	78
Goals	0
Assists	0

6

NATHAN AKE

After a highly impressive loan spell at Bournemouth in the first half of the season had caught the eye, Nathan Ake returned to Chelsea in January and was reliable as ever when called upon.

Three of his five appearances came in the FA Cup, including a mature display when asked to start on the left of the back three against Tottenham in the semi-final at Wembley. His only start in the league came in the penultimate game of the campaign against Watford, where he had impressed during a loan spell the previous season.

Ake may not be the tallest of defenders, but his mobility, spring and composure make him a very difficult proposition for all kinds of striker. Such is his adaptability and his focus that the left-footer is more than comfortable playing as a full-back, a wing-back, a centre-back or a central midfielder, where he was used in his initial foray into the first team back in 2012/13.

Now the Academy graduate is looking to continue his development into a first-team player, having rarely put a foot wrong so far.

NATHAN AKE	
Position: Defender	
Date of birth: 18.02.95	
Place of birth: The Hague, Holland	
2016/17 PREMIER LEAGUE	
Appearances	1+1
Minutes	109
Goals	0
Assists	1

2

BRANISLAV IVANOVIC

Nine years after joining the club where he won every major domestic and European title, Branislav Ivanovic departed in January.

The Serbian defender – who was a Premier League champion with Chelsea in 2009/10 and 2014/15 – had started the first six league games of the 2016/17 title-winning season at right-back in a four-man defence.

However, after the fifth and sixth of those fixtures ended in defeat, Antonio Conte changed the system and Ivanovic was one of the players to lose his starting position.

He made seven further league appearances from the bench between October and January before departing for Zenit St Petersburg. He signed off with a goal in his last Chelsea game, a 4-0 win over Brentford in the FA Cup.

BRANISLAV IVANOVIC	
Position: Defender	
Date of birth: 22.02.84	
Place of birth: Sremska Mitrovica, Serbia	
2016/17 PREMIER LEAGUE	
Appearances	6+7
Minutes	643
Goals	0
Assists	0

14

RUBEN LOFTUS-CHEEK

The 2016/17 season was Ruben Loftus-Cheek's third in the first-team squad and the Chelsea Academy graduate, who has been at the club since the age of eight, made six substitute appearances in our Premier League campaign.

The youngster – who turned 21 halfway through the season – also made four starts in cup competition and was introduced to a new role as a forward by Antonio Conte when he partnered Michy Batshuayi up front in the early rounds of the EFL Cup.

RUBEN LOFTUS-CHEEK	
Position: Midfielder	
Date of birth: 23.01.96	
Place of birth: Lewisham	
2016/17 PREMIER LEAGUE	
Appearances	0+6
Minutes	98
Goals	0
Assists	0

1

ASMIR BEGOVIC

After being called upon frequently during his first season at Chelsea following his 2015 arrival, Asmir Begovic found Premier League minutes harder to come by during his second campaign at the Bridge.

Having spent five-and-a-half years with Stoke City, he made 25 appearances in his first Chelsea season and kept eight of the team's 14 clean sheets.

However, a lack of playing time in 2016/17 led to speculation regarding his future during the January transfer window, when Antonio Conte agreed he could leave if a quality replacement could be found.

That did not happen and the decision to keep Begovic was vindicated when he was required for our visit to Old Trafford following an injury to Thibaut Courtois, and he was also selected against Watford. The majority of his minutes came in the domestic cup competitions, though, as he started three games in both the EFL Cup and FA Cup.

In May it was announced that Begovic would be leaving for Bournemouth, where he would be first-choice keeper. No one at the club could begrudge this likeable and talented player that opportunity.

ASMIR BEGOVIC	
Position: Goalkeeper	
Date of birth: 20.06.87	
Place of birth: Trebinje, SFR Yugoslavia	
2016/17 PREMIER LEAGUE	
Appearances	2
Minutes	194
Clean sheets	0

8

OSCAR

Having won the Premier League, Europa League and League Cup during his first four campaigns with the Blues, it looked as though Oscar would have an integral role to play in our push for major honours in the 2016/17 campaign.

Antonio Conte's arrival in the summer led to a deeper role for the Brazilian, who had previously been deployed as an energetic No10 who pressed high up the pitch, and he started each of our first five Premier League matches as the Blues made a middling start to the campaign.

However, the switch to a 3-4-2-1 system at the beginning of October limited starting opportunities for the two-time Goal of the Season winner, who was restricted to cameos from the substitutes' bench. His final start for the club came in an EFL Cup defeat to West Ham United that month.

In January, Oscar moved to Chinese Super League club Shanghai SIPG, managed by former Chelsea boss Andre Villas-Boas.

Skilful and tenacious, Oscar was always highly regarded by fans, players and staff during his time as a Blue, scoring 38 times in 203 appearances.

OSCAR	
Position: Midfielder	
Date of birth: 09.09.91	
Place of birth: Sao Paulo, Brazil	
2016/17 PREMIER LEAGUE	
Appearances	5+4
Minutes	477
Goals	0
Assists	1

29

NATHANIEL CHALOBAH

We may well look back at 2016/17 in years to come as the season that Nathaniel Chalobah made the breakthrough as a fully fledged member of the Chelsea first-team squad. Hopes are high for his future in the game having captained our Academy sides to trophies and spending the previous few campaigns gaining experience on loan, and Antonio Conte identified the youngster early on in pre-season as someone ready to play a role in his side.

First came Chalobah's Chelsea debut, as a substitute in the thrilling 4-2 extra-time win over Leicester City in the League Cup, followed by his first start in another victory, this time against Peterborough United in the FA Cup third round.

However, it was in the Premier League that the 22-year-old made his biggest impact, frequently being used from the bench by Conte to change our shape and add an extra man in midfield when holding a lead in the second half. It was on one such occasion the highlight of his season arrived, again against Leicester, as his silky and elegant spinning back-heel set up Victor Moses to complete the 3-0 victory.

NATHANIEL CHALOBAH	
Position: Defender/Midfielder	
Date of birth: 12.12.94	
Place of birth: Freetown, Sierra Leone	
2016/17 PREMIER LEAGUE	
Appearances	1+9
Minutes	200
Goals	0
Assists	0

Gary Cahill jumps on top of his team-mates as they celebrate N'Golo Kanté's goal in the Blues' 4-0 victory over Manchester United

CHELSEA FC AWARDS 2017

CHELSEA FC AWARDS 2017

The Blues' outstanding performers were recognised as the club celebrated the end of a successful season at the Chelsea FC Awards.

Players, staff and supporters gathered at Battersea Evolution in south-west London for the event, which was hosted by television and radio presenter Jeremy Vine and comedian Omid Djalili.

But the star of the show was Eden Hazard, who received both the Yokohama Chelsea Player of the Year and Goal of the Season awards.

The Belgian winger became only the second person – after club legend Frank Lampard – to be voted our

Eden Hazard, on stage alongside Antonio Conte and host Jeremy Vine, with his Player of the Year trophy

N'Golo Kanté speaks to Omid Djalili after being named the Chelsea Players' Player of the Year

Player of the Year by supporters on three occasions, having previously won back-to-back awards in 2014 and 2015.

Hazard enjoyed his most prolific season yet in the Premier League, scoring 16 times as we marched towards the title, so it was fitting that he was also presented with the award for the best goal.

His weaving run at Stamford Bridge in the derby against Arsenal came out on top ahead of Nemanja Matic's Wembley pile-driver in the FA Cup semi-final.

N'Golo Kanté, meanwhile, won his fourth major individual honour of the season after being chosen as Chelsea Players' Player of the Year. The French midfielder had already been named Player of the

CHELSEA FC AWARDS 2017

Year by the Premier League, Football Writers' Association and Professional Footballers' Association.

Chelsea Ladies' squad members – on the way to being crowned FA WSL Spring Series Champions – were also in attendance in Battersea, with the Player of the Year award going to England international Karen Carney.

Under-18s manager Jody Morris, himself a Blues youth system graduate, was on hand to congratulate his players on a great campaign after they secured a fourth successive FA Youth Cup triumph as well as the southern and national league titles.

Midfielder Mason Mount, who scored a combined 10 goals in 39 appearances for our development

Mason Mount

Emma Hayes and Karen Carney

CHELSEA FC AWARDS 2017

Assistant first-team coach Steve Holland was presented with a framed collection of photos as a goodbye gift from the club

squad and Under-18s last term, was named as the adidas Chelsea Academy Player of the Year.

The evening – which also raised money for the Chelsea Foundation and Plan International – was also an occasion to look back at previous successes, as the club bid a fond farewell to John Terry and Steve Holland.

Assistant first-team coach Holland was presented with a framed collection of photos marking his eight years at Stamford Bridge before he departed with the best wishes of everybody at the club to take up a new full-time role as part of the England national team's coaching staff.

Departing captain Terry, our most successful player of all time, brought proceedings to an emotional close with a speech thanking all the fans, team-mates and staff who have contributed to his incredible 22-year Chelsea career.

Claudio Ranieri – the first manager to hand him the skipper's armband – made a special presentation on behalf of the club as a standing ovation for our captain, leader and legend brought the curtain down on the 2016/17 season.

John Terry receives a silver trophy commemorating the number of appearances he made for the Blues from former Chelsea manager Claudio Ranieri

ROLL OF HONOUR

PLAYER OF THE YEAR

1967	Peter Bonetti
1968	Charlie Cooke
1969	David Webb
1970	John Hollins
1971	John Hollins
1972	David Webb
1973	Peter Osgood
1974	Gary Locke
1975	Charlie Cooke
1976	Ray Wilkins
1977	Ray Wilkins
1978	Micky Droy
1979	Tommy Langley
1980	Clive Walker
1981	Petar Borota
1982	Mike Fillery
1983	Joey Jones
1984	Pat Nevin
1985	David Speedie
1986	Eddie Niedzwiecki
1987	Pat Nevin
1988	Tony Dorigo
1989	Graham Roberts
1990	Ken Monkou
1991	Andy Townsend
1992	Paul Elliott
1993	Frank Sinclair
1994	Steve Clarke
1995	Erland Johnsen
1996	Ruud Gullit
1997	Mark Hughes
1998	Dennis Wise
1999	Gianfranco Zola
2000	Dennis Wise
2001	John Terry
2002	Carlo Cudicini
2003	Gianfranco Zola
2004	Frank Lampard
2005	Frank Lampard
2006	John Terry
2007	Michael Essien
2008	Joe Cole
2009	Frank Lampard
2010	Didier Drogba
2011	Petr Cech
2012	Juan Mata
2013	Juan Mata
2014	Eden Hazard
2015	Eden Hazard
2016	Willian
2017	Eden Hazard

PLAYERS' PLAYER OF THE YEAR

2006	Claude Makelele
2007	Didier Drogba
2008	Ricardo Carvalho
2009	Ashley Cole
2010	Florent Malouda
2011	Ashley Cole
2012	Ramires
2013	Juan Mata
2014	Cesar Azpilicueta
2015	Eden Hazard
2016	Willian
2017	N'Golo Kanté

ACADEMY PLAYER OF THE YEAR

2015	Dominic Solanke
2016	Fikayo Tomori
2017	Mason Mount

CHELSEA LADIES' PLAYER OF THE YEAR

2015	Eniola Aluko
2016	Katie Chapman
2017	Karen Carney

GOAL OF THE SEASON

2007	Essien v Arsenal (h)
2008	Belletti v Tottenham (h)
2009	Essien v Barcelona (h)
2010	A Cole v Sunderland (h)
2011	Ramires v Man City (h)
2012	Ramires v Barcelona (a)
2013	Oscar v Juventus (h)
2014	Baker v Arsenal U21s (a)
2015	Oscar v QPR (h)
2016	Hazard v Tottenham (h)
2017	Hazard v Arsenal (h)

Scroll of Honour

Compiled from loyal fans who subscribed to Chelsea FC: Champions 2016/17. They take their place alongside the manager and every player who contributed to our successful Premier League campaign

THE MANAGER & PLAYERS

ANTONIO CONTE

OLA AINA
NATHAN AKE
MARCOS ALONSO
CESAR AZPILICUETA
MICHY BATSHUAYI
ASMIR BEGOVIC
GARY CAHILL
NATHANIEL CHALOBAH
THIBAUT COURTOIS
DIEGO COSTA
EDUARDO
CESC FÀBREGAS
EDEN HAZARD
BRANISLAV IVANOVIC
N'GOLO KANTE
KENEDY
RUBEN LOFTUS-CHEEK
DAVID LUIZ
NEMANJA MATIC
VICTOR MOSES
OSCAR
PEDRO
JOHN TERRY
WILLIAN
KURT ZOUMA

SCROLL OF HONOUR

THE FANS

MUHAMMAD AIMIN AISANUDDIN ABD MANAF
MUHAMMAD AZRIL BIN ABD RAHMAN
TEHMINA AHMED
DARWEESH AL-SAIDI
DAMILOLA ALAWODE
SARAH AND MOHAMAD
ALJUMAIE
SALEH ALMUKAIMI
STEEN HURUP ANDERSEN
STEVE ASHBY
DAVID ASPINALL
COLIN AUBURY
DAVID AUSTIN
REECE BACHELOR
IAN BAILEY
TONY BAKER
DAVID BALDERSTONE
JOSEPH MIZZI
SIMON BANYARD
EMILY BARKER
DAVID BARR
DAVID BARRETT
MELVIN BARTOLOME
MICHAEL BATE
CHESTER BATES
BHISHAM BATRA
DAVID BAZELY
HARRY AND HONEY BEAR
DALE JONATHAN BECKMANN
JUSTIN BENNETT
LYN BENNETT
LUKE BERWICK
EASHAN BHAN
EASHAN BHAN
DOUGLAS BIDGOOD
RAY BILLINGHURST
MARTYN BIRCH
ALAN BITMEAD
JIMMY BLOCK
ANDY BOARD
BERNIE BOARD
WILLIAM BOLTON
STAN BORKOWSKI
CAROLE AND JON BOWERS
STEFAN BRABENETZ
SARAH BRAIN
ANDREW JON BRAY
PHILIP BREWER
HOLLY BROOKS
MARC BROOKS
KEVIN BROWN
PETE BULL
ANTHONY BURCHELL
BILLY BURCHER
PAUL BURCHER
STEVEN BURROWS
LIZ BUSSEY
MICHAEL BUTEUX
HARRY CAFFELL
GRAEME CALDWELL
ZAC CAMMERMAN
JOHN CAVANAGH
RICKI CHANDLER
AARON CHILDERS
ALEX CHIN-A-FAT
GRACE GALLAGHER CHIN
SCOTT CHISHOLM
CHRIS CLAYDEN
CHRISTOPHER COLDWELL
PETER COLLINS
JOSEPH E. COMPTON IV
PATRICK E. COOKE
LEWIS COOPER
COL AND SUE COWLEY
DEREK COX
JOHN EDWARD COX
VERA COYNE
KYLE CRAWFORD
JOHN CURTIS
ALAN DAVIDSON
LIZZIE DAVIS
ALLEN DAY
BJORN DE PAEPE
CHARLES DEACON
SUSAN DEASY
YASEEN DEEN
JIM DELARGY
PHIL DENTY
JOHN DERRIG
RUSSELL DICKINSON
MORGAN DOCHERTY
JACK A. F. DORMER
ERIC STEWART DUFF
IAN DUMOND
PAUL DURIE
KEITH DYE
ROBERT DYE
COLIN EAST
SAM EASTON
GARY EASY
MOHAMED EL-ALFY
PHILIP ELLIOTT
JONATHAN EVANS
DAVID EZEKIEL
JACKIE FACEY
THE LUMSDON FAMILY
THE HARSTON FAMILY
THE GOULD FAMILY
JOHN FARMER
STEPHEN FARROW
CAMILO FERNANDES
NEIL FIELDING
LES FLANAGAN
ALICE G. FLETCHER
BRUNO FREEMAN
NIGEL FROST
MASAHIKO FUJINAGA

THE FANS

JACK FUKE
JOHN GAGE
RIC GALE
JOSEPH PETER GEDLING
TONY GIBSON
CLIFF AND DIANE GIDDENS
ALEXANDER JAMES GILBERT
MICHAEL GILLESPIE
KEVIN GOLDING
BRIAN GOLDSBURY
KATIE GOLDSMITH
MATTHEW GOODSON
ROB GORDON
PATRICK GORDON-BROWN
GINETTE GOWER
RYAN GREANEY
ANDREW GREEN
MARK GREENAWAY
PAUL GREENAWAY
MICK GRIST
GARRY B. GROVE
SHIKHA GUJADHUR
LEWIS HALSEY
JEZ HARE
KERRY "KEZZA" HARRISON
NICHOLAS "CFCNICK" HARRISON
SALLY HARRISON
ALAN HARRISON
AMANDA HART
RICHARD HART
KERI HAWKINS
BETHANY HAWTHORNE
REO HAYASHI
JOHN HAYES
KALLE HEIMO
HARRI HEMMI
GARETH HENRY
MAURICE HERRING
RICHARD HEWITT
CHRIS HIGGINS
MARTIN HILDITCH
ROY HINCHLIFFE
ANDREW JOSEPH HINRICHS
ROSS HISLOP
CHARLIE HOLLOWAY
CONOR HOSFORD
THOMAS HOSKINS
ZHENFEI HU
BILL HUBERT
CASSIUS HUDSON
EMILY HUE
IAN HURDLE-ROWE
OLIVIA INCE
STEPHEN INGLETON
MATT JACKSON
SHENICK DHONI JAIN
SHIRLEY JARDINE
BENNY STEPHEN JEAL
SIMON JENKINS
JON JENKINS
NIGEL JESSOP
FABIAN JIANNIOULIS
JAN JOHANSEN
COLIN B. JOLLIFF
ALAN JOLLY
BEN AND HARRY JONES
DENNIS M. JONES
MATTHEW H. JONES
DEREK JONES
KEVIN JOYCE
RANNVEIG KARLSDÓTTIR
JAMES KENNEDY
SJAAK KENTERS
OLIVER KERSHAW
JAMIE KIDD
LIAM KING
STEVEN G. KINGE
TRACY KIRK
PETER KITCHEN
JAMES KLONOWSKI
PETER KNIGHT
TERUHITO "TERRY" KOMATSU
CHARLIE KOZIK-ROWE
IAN LANGRIDGE
SZILÁDI LÁSZLÓ
WALLACE LAW
SU JIN LEE
CONRAD LEIGH
LEO G. LEVENIUS
YVES LEZY
TIM LIDDIARD
JAMIE LOSSOS
BENJAMIN PETER MACARTAN
SPENCER MALONEY
JOSEPH MALONEY
DOMINIC MALONEY
MARIA MALVATANI
PAUL MANGAN
SIRA MANOROM
MICHAEL MANZI
BENJAMIN MANZI
THEODORE MANZI
PERCIVAL MANZI
HELENA FLORENCE MARCEL
BARBARA MARKOVIC
MIKE MARLOW
IIKKA MARVIA
ROB MASON
ADAM MATARI
IAN MAYERS
MILAN MAYES
WILLIAM MCALISTER
BEN McCARTHY
JOSEPH McCRORY
BUDDY McGUINNESS
KATH McKENZIE
SEAN MEHMET